THE LGBTQIA+ COMMUNITY
and BETRAYAL

Heterophobia vs. Homophobia And How the Alphabet Mob Is Erasing Heterosexuality and Trying to Bully Us "Straights" into the "Closet" From Tolerance to Equality to Heterophobia

K.B. LEWIS

authorHOUSE'

AuthorHouse™
1663 Liberty Drive
Bloomington, IN 47403
www.authorhouse.com
Phone: 833-262-8899

Published by AuthorHouse 01/19/2024

ISBN: 979-8-8230-2097-8 (sc)
ISBN: 979-8-8230-2096-1 (e)

Library of Congress Control Number: 2024901495

Print information available on the last page.

Any people depicted in stock imagery provided by Getty Images are models,
and such images are being used for illustrative purposes only.
Certain stock imagery © Getty Images.

This book is printed on acid-free paper.

CONTENTS

The Betrayal: How The Lgbtqia Community Has Negatively Taken Over The United STATE LGBTQIA+ Is Trying To Bully Us 'Straights' Into The "Closet"; Lgbtqia+ Erasing Heterosexuality Out Of Existence

The LGBTQIA community does not get to ram their identity or ideology down our throats and bully heterosexuals into the closet. We get to decide our own identity and beliefs.

The LGBTQIA community has betrayed the heterosexual community and burned the bridge behind them, meaning that there is no turning back. Why? Because they are hell-bent on taking down and destroying the heterosexual community's way of thinking and believing, and its lifestyle, in order to advance their homosexual agenda and complete their societal takeover of the United States. From grade school (with the transgender sexual curriculum), to corporate America (Bud Light and transgender influencer Dylan Mulvaney), to Disney changing and altering its movies to fit the LGBTQIA vision, to parents being labeled as domestic terrorists for questioning school board members about teachers trying to recruit and indoctrinate their children, to children as young as ten making their own life-altering decisions without their parents' permission or knowledge and permanently changing their biological gender, the LGBTQIA community is betraying the heterosexual community. Why do I say it's a betrayal? Because the LGBTQIA community started off by asking the heterosexual community to be more tolerant, and once they got their tolerance, they asked for equality. Once they got their equality, they demanded the legalization of gay marriage, and once they got that, they demanded to become a protected class. Once they got their protected class status, they gained more rights than the heterosexual community. And once they got those, they turned on the heterosexual community and began separating themselves from it because they found themselves being too much like the heterosexuals by losing their gay status and identity, which is the one thing that made them different and gave them significance. Since they have gotten what they asked for, including all the rights that the heterosexual community has and more, they are now trying to recruit and indoctrinate the heterosexual community, conforming them to their lifestyle and erasing the heterosexual lifestyle out of existence. The LGBTQIA community first gained the heterosexual community's trust, then they turned on them and stabbed them in the back. Now they are trying to dismantle everything about the heterosexual lifestyle. They are trying to make heterosexuals bow down to the LGBTQIA community's will and live under their umbrella and according to their beliefs. It was a deceptive plot followed through with an underline plan to gain power for themselves and then destroy the core of the heterosexual community.

This is heterophobia and a total betrayal. What happened to tolerance?

You may be saying to yourself right now, *How did gay people betray straight people? All they want is to be accepted and to be treated equally and fairly?* I just said something that seems negative toward the LGBTQIA community, and this is likely going to trigger many people into believing that this is homophobia, which accusation is the weapon of choice they use to silence and censor heterosexuals into submission or compliance when they can't, or don't, or won't debate the issues head-on or when they can't dispute the heterosexuals or measure up to them. To address this point, let's take a trip down memory lane and find out how we got to where we are today in society, a point where heterosexuals are afraid to speak their minds or have their own opinions. The gay community first said that they only wanted the heterosexual community to be more tolerant of them and their behavior. They wanted more inclusiveness and the ability to integrate and blend into society so that they wouldn't be targets of discrimination or hate crimes. There is nothing wrong with that. Everyone should be respectful of others and not be abusive or violent toward the LGBTQIA community. There is no room for that kind of behavior in our society. So, over the years we as a society started to accept more and more of the LGBTQIA community's lifestyle. We as a society started to put laws into place, such as laws opposed to hate crimes, in order to stop violence and abuses toward the LGBTQIA community. The LGBTQIA community then was given protected class status, which emboldened them seeing as they now had more rights and were subjected to better treatment than every other group, including the heterosexual community as a whole. You may be saying right now, *How do they have more rights than the heterosexual community?* Well, I'll give you an example.

If someone physically attacks a member of the LGBTQIA community, this is considered a hate crime. The person will go to prison and possibly get a stiffer sentence or stronger punishment than if he or she had attacked or assaulted another heterosexual. Now let's reverse this scenario. What if a member of the LGBTQIA community physically attacks someone in the heterosexual community? Is that considered a hate crime? No, it's not. Why not? Because the LGBTQIA community has protected class status, which the heterosexual community doesn't have.

Here is an example: I was watching *Fox News* on August 8, 2023, and they aired a story about Riley Gaines, the female swimming champion who has become an advocate for female rights and is against biological males who identify as women competing in women's sports—a.k.a. transgender women. She is the woman who lost her title to the transgender woman Lia Thomas, a biological man who is pretending to be a woman. I say "pretend" because this transgender woman still has a penis, which means that he is a man. Riley Gaines was going to a Texas statehouse building for the ceremonial signing of a bill that would protect women's sports from being infiltrated by biological males. The ceremony was being held by the governor of Texas Greg Abbott. As Riley Gaines was walking into the ceremony, she and others, including small children, were approached and attacked by some LGBTQIA community members and LGBTQIA sympathizers. They were yelling, screaming profanities, and hitting Gaines and the others with objects. These LGBTQIA people were spitting in Riley Gaines's and others' faces, which is assault. Now what do you think happened to the LGBTQIA community members who attacked Riley and the others? You guessed it: absolutely nothing.

They were given a free pass to assault members of the heterosexual community.

Now what do you think would have happened if members of the heterosexual community had spit in the faces of members of the LGBTQIA community and thrown objects and yelled hateful profanity at them? You've guessed it again: they would have been arrested and charged with a hate crime. Now why weren't these LGBTQIA members not arrested and punished for their heterophobic behavior? It's because the LGBTQIA community is protected and the heterosexual community is not. Therefore, the LGBTQIA community has more rights than the heterosexual community, which is unfair. This proves my point and serves as explanation for why I correctly label the LGBTQIA community as the "alphabet mob." Many (not all) members of the LGBTQIA community believe that they are entitled to attack and assault members of the heterosexual community and that there should be no punishment for their criminal behavior. They believe that the ends (social domination) justify the means (physical assault). They believe that they can do no wrong as long as what they are doing is acting against the heterosexual community only. This is a betrayal of the heterosexual community. Remember that the LGBTQIA community asked the heterosexual community for tolerance, and now that they have gotten it, they have been emboldened and feel entitled to assault, harass, and bully the heterosexual community at will.

I'm part of Generation X, the last generation not to have been brainwashed or indoctrinated by the leftists and the LGBTQIA community. Where I come from, if someone spits in your face, it's the ultimate sign of disrespect. This action is worse than hitting a person in the face with your fist. Why hasn't the LGBTQIA community and its leaders, or the mainstream news media outlets, condemned this negative behavior? I'll tell you why. It's because they are all on the same side. Many news media outlets are silently siding with the LGBTQIA community and approve of their behavior. These outlets are very liberal, and some are Far Left advocates. They don't want to punish their own, because they benefit from this type of negative behavior. The mainstream news media don't want to show the LGBTQIA community members in a negative light. They don't air the types of stories where people from the LGBTQIA community are assaulting heterosexuals, because they don't want heterosexual people to know about the LGBTQIA plot and the LGBTQIA plan, as this would go against their cause and their agenda, which is to erase heterosexuality and replace it with homosexuality. The leftists want to tear down everything heterosexual and replace it with the LGBTQIA community's version, things that gain their stamp of approval.

The LGBTQIA community have infringed on the rights of heterosexuals in every area of our society, including our government and law enforcement agencies, such the Department of Justice (DOJ) and the Federal Bureau of Investigation (FBI), which has put parents who attend certain school board meetings on the domestic terrorist watch list. Think about that for a minute. The DOJ and the FBI are calling parents who want to protect their own children from harmful content from the LGBTQIA community "terrorists." It's a massive form of intimidation by our government and our law enforcement agencies on behalf of the leftist LGBTQIA community. Again, where do the mainstream news media stand on this issue? Why aren't they getting the word out to the people, which is their job according to the US Constitution? They are there to protect against and stop government overreach and to allow for freedom of speech. I remember when former president Donald Trump called out the mainstream news media for being the "enemy of the people." Now

I know what he means by that. If the mainstream news media don't give the American people true information, then how can we make a proper, sound decision on who is the right person to lead this great nation? That's the problem. The LGBTQIA community, and the Democratic Party, and the Far Leftists are one and the same. There is no difference between them. So, the mainstream media are only going to air what the Democrats and the Far Leftists want the people to see and hear, which is their message only. That way, they can shape the minds and opinions of the people, getting them to think and believe the way they want them to, that is, brainwash them. A person can only make a sound decision based upon the information that he or she has been given. I watch a number of different news outlets because I want to get the full picture and also because I now understand that the people behind the mainstream news media are humans just like the rest of us and they have chosen sides. Many of them has chosen to side with the Far Leftists and the Democratic Party, and not necessarily the American people.

Now I mentioned former president Trump for a reason. It's in regard to freedom of speech, something that we all have a right to as Americans. The DOJ, which reports to the president of the United States, is prosecuting former president Trump for freedom of speech violations. Now I'm not a Republican or a Democrat, but I know right and wrong when I see it. I also know bias when I see it. And I know when the government is trying to take away Americans' First Amendment rights, that is, our freedom of speech. If you oppose former president Trump for whatever reason, you had better be careful what you ask for, because you just may get it. Because if the current government successfully prosecutes Trump for these alleged crimes, then the removal of your right to freedom of speech is next. Since when has stating one's opinions been a crime? This is a slippery slope we are going down when the government can put a person in jail for saying something that is protected by the First Amendment. The message this sends is that if the government doesn't like what a person says, or if a person disagrees with the government or its agenda, then the government has the right to put the person in jail. What kind of country are we living in today? This sounds like something you'd expect from China or Russia or some other dictatorial country such as North Korea or Iran, and not the United States. Our freedom of speech is what separates us from these communist (or in the case of Iran, theocratic) countries. And this way of behaving sounds just like the LGBTQIA community, which is trying to shut down free speech for anyone who legitimately opposes them. Remember that if someone is trying to shut down the rights of one group, they are going to try to shut down your rights too. This street goes both ways. If you believe that this is right, fair, and honest because your party is currently in power now, remember that one day your party will be out of power, and then your throat will be under the foot of the same dictatorship that you believed in when it favored you. Now it will be against you because you didn't fight for the freedom of speech for others, which means for everyone.

So, heterosexuals, take a stand, because right now the LGBTQIA community has more rights than you. Get it? Even Ne-Yo, the famous R&B singer, came out on July 2023 and said that he believes it is wrong for the LGBTQIA community to make permanent decisions about sexual orientation for underage children. He said that things have gone too far with the LGBTQIA community's wanting to give five-year-olds the right to make the decision to have a permanent sex change operation without their parents' knowledge or consent. Then his publicist came out and made a statement on his behalf, a so-called apology. Then Ne-Yo came back after his publicist's statement to correct the record, saying that it was not his statement, but his publicist's, and that he still stood by his original statement, which was in opposition to granting a five-year-old the right to make a life-altering decision about his or her gender without his or her parents' permission. Well, you guessed it: the alphabet mob launched an attack against Ne-Yo, bullying him and trying to intimidate him into bowing down to their demand to help them in carrying out their agenda, which is to erase heterosexuality, and also calling him a homophobe, which is just not true. This is the LGBTQIA version of sexual discrimination, that is, heterophobia, in full effect.

The message here is that no one is allowed to state their own opinion, or even mention facts, if those opinions and facts—no matter if they are right—oppose the agenda of the LGBTQIA community. Ne-Yo was just stating the facts and his own opinion on the matter. His publicist is clearly a LGBTQIA sympathizer, or at least is afraid of the alphabet mob's attacks, and was trying to backdoor Ne-Yo, meaning go behind his back and make it appear as if Ne-Yo had changed his opinion and now understood that he was wrong for going against the leftist LGBTQIA community. The publicist, who feared the alphabet mob, was trying to indoctrinate Ne-Yo for the purposes of recruiting him as an activist for the LGBTQIA community's cause without his knowledge or approval. Ne-Yo shut down that lie, a clear act of deception by his own publicist.

This is a way that members of the LGBTQIA community gain power and advance their cause of erasing heterosexuality, by turning celebrities or people who oppose them into advocates for LGBTQIA. Once the LGBTQIA community calls you a homophobe, you are left to defend yourself from the alphabet mob, who will try to get you canceled from certain platforms or try to get you fired from your job. Then they can extort you like an organized crime boss by holding the prospect of cancellation over your head and forcing you to join them in their cause if you wish not to be canceled. Extortion is a Mafia-style tactic that is used like a threat to bully a person into submission. (I'll discuss the other types of tactics later in chapter 5.) It's kind of like, "Do what we want you to do, or else we will destroy your life."

Once the alphabet mob gets you to bow down and apologize for your remarks, they turn you into an advocate to fight their cause, which is to take down heterosexuality and replace it with homosexuality, which goes against your personal values and beliefs and your own heterosexuality. This is not only a betrayal but also a clever and deceptive way of getting heterosexuals to join the LGBTQIA cause to erase heterosexuality. This is what the LGBTQIA community tried to do with Ne-Yo. But it didn't work because he stood his ground, as should everyone who is heterosexual.

Heterosexuals, this is what I mean when I say we must take a stand. Ne-Yo took a stand to protect his rights and other parents' rights, even if what he did ultimately delivered a blow to his music career. He knows that our right to freedom of speech is being taking away from us, that the LGBTQIA community is trying to erase heterosexuality, and that they are going after your children to make them more like them and less like you. The LGBTQIA community has betrayed you, and now they want to change the United States into a LGBTQIA society where heterosexuals are no longer the ruling class, having been replaced by members of the LGBTQIA community as part of the new world order. This is a betrayal. Now the people this new protected class status have overwhelmed the heterosexual community and are attempting to take over our society in the name of equality and with the threat that anyone who opposes this move will be called homophobic, extorted, and bullied into becoming LGBTQIA advocates against their own best interests. There are many leaders in the LGBTQIA community who have been emboldened and are leading their constituent groups like a mob in order to shut down certain speakers who are heterosexual on college and university campuses and other places because they have deemed themselves as righteous and the only voices worthy of being heard. And if anyone opposes them, questions them, debates them, or even stands up for his or her own rights against them in any way, then they will try to shame the person, bully him or her into silence, censor and make him or her submit. The message, then, is that all heterosexuals should silence themselves or self-censor so as to avoid offending the LGBTQIA community and, therefore, be destroyed by them. Now you may be asking yourself when this divide occurred, when this betrayal happened, and how the LGBTQIA community went from advocating for tolerance to becoming a heterophobic dictatorship.

The divide happened right after the Supreme Court ruled that homosexuals had the right to adopt children and the gay marriage bill was passed. This made it so that homosexuals could be just like heterosexuals—and therein lies the problem.

Now you may be asking yourself why the LGBTQIA community wanted to be divided from the heterosexual community, as you may have thought that they wanted to integrate with the heterosexual community and be seen as equal to heterosexuals. Those were their objectives at first, until they found themselves becoming too much like heterosexuals, to the point that they felt they had lost their gay status or even their gay identity, which was the one thing that gave their lives any significance, imparting to them a sense of importance because they were different—and their getting a lot of attention as a result. Being homosexual or transgender made them different, and they liked being different and unlike others, meaning heterosexuals. When they lost that attention for being gay, they felt that they had lost themselves, which is why they intentionally drove a wedge between themselves and the heterosexual community, because they wanted to be accepted by the heterosexual community but didn't want to be exactly *like* the heterosexual community. Their gay status gave them the clear sense that they had their own identity, which gave them victimhood status, which brought them attention, which was important to them and separated them from heterosexuals. And they didn't want to lose that status. Then eventually they chose to rebel because that was the only way they could achieve separation from the heterosexual community—have that divide and maintain their sense of individuality and their gay status. They didn't like what the heterosexual community stood for or its lifestyle. If you don't like a group's lifestyle and you don't want to be like them, what does that mean? It means that on some level you hate them. And if you hate a person or a group of people just because of who they are, then that is a phobia. In this case, who is the phobia against? Heterosexuals. Which makes most (not all) members of the LGBTQIA community heterophobic.

Now I know some people are going to say that LGBTQIA people don't hate heterosexuals, they just want to be themselves, which means gay, trans, or what have you. However, remember that their reason for not wanting to be like heterosexuals is that they dislike the heterosexual lifestyle. And if you dislike something, it means that on some level you hate it. Therefore, you are going to do things that oppose that lifestyle and are in favor of your own lifestyle. This is exactly what we have going on today in 2023. For example, many members of the LGBTQIA community pretend that they are unable to define what a woman is. Why? Because they don't like the fact that the dictionary definition doesn't match their version of what a woman is. They want to erase heterosexual women from society and replace them with their own version of a woman, which is the transgender female, that is, a biological male. If you hate the idea that the standard for a woman is a heterosexual woman, and if your aim is to eliminate heterosexual women into nonexistence, then you hate heterosexual women. So, that's heterophobia.

Because the LGBTQIA community fears that if the standard for womanhood is a heterosexual woman and therefore that their version of a woman will not be accepted, they decided that the best course of action was to refuse to acknowledge heterosexual women altogether. That's a betrayal because the gay community asked the heterosexual community for their tolerance and for equality, which they were given, along with acceptance, and now the LGBTQIA community is throwing heterosexual women under the bus, giving them the middle finger, and telling them to go to hell. That's heterophobia, which is a knife in the backs of heterosexual women, who have been bitten by the LGBTQIA snake. Now remember, the reason the LGBTQIA community turned on heterosexual women was because they wished to intentionally divide themselves from the heterosexual community, remaining separate but being equal. The LGBTQIA community now had to be against the heterosexual community but at the same time integrate with them. And after they achieved their holy grail, which was gay marriage, they no longer had a use for heterosexual women or heterosexuality.

Now it doesn't matter what the heterosexual community has to say about it. The LGBTQIA community is protected against the heterosexual community, which reminds me of where the betrayal of the heterosexual community started. Now the LGBTQIA community have power and higher status than the heterosexual community because they are a so-called "protected class" and on an equal playing field, which has emboldened them to come out of the closet and start making demands on and setting terms for the heterosexual community. This is where the heterophobia comes in. The attitude changed to, *We don't like the heterosexual lifestyle, so you should become more like us and adopt the LGBTQIA community lifestyle.* This is where the LGBTQIA community flipped the script on the heterosexual community, betraying them after having secured their acceptance and tolerance and now beginning to erase them from society. This was made possible by their protected class status and originated from their fear of becoming more like heterosexuals than homosexuals and, therefore, rebelling. Many members of the LGBTQIA community have hidden disdain and disgust for the heterosexual community and don't like or even hate the heterosexual lifestyle because it's the direct opposite of the LGBTQIA community lifestyle. How can the LGBTQIA community not hate the heterosexual lifestyle when most everything in our society is built on and caters to heterosexuals and when most things considered gay actually go against the LGBTQIA lifestyle. Gays see things opposite from straights. I imagine some may say that I just made a homophobic comment by saying that heterosexuals are straight. If so, that would only prove my claim that members of the LGBTQIA hate the heterosexual lifestyle. I say this because it would show that they envy it, and if you envy something, then you in essence hate it. Members of the LGBTQIA community hate heterosexuality because society views it as better than, or the standard over, homosexuality. That's why I say they are heterophobic. Because they want the homosexual lifestyle to be both the standard and the dominant lifestyle and not the heterosexual lifestyle.

Don't believe it? Then explain why many members of the LGBTQIA community want to change our school curriculums, from grade school to college, in order to implement their own agenda and promote their own lifestyle instead of that of heterosexuals. Explain why they don't want to acknowledge what a heterosexual woman is, and at the same time replace the standard of a heterosexual woman with a transgender woman, that is, a biological male, which is their version of a woman. Explain why they want to change the pronouns they use to identify themselves, moving away from the gender-based pronouns *he*, *she*, *him*, and *her* and toward the gender-ambiguous pronouns *they* and *them*, their way of identifying either male or female, to replace the heterosexual version. Explain why they want to stop calling mothers "pregnant women" and start calling them "birthing people." Which is their version of a pregnant woman. Explain why they are saying that a man can get pregnant. It's because they want their version of a man to be the standard, which is a gay woman who so-called "identifies" as a man. They want every part of our society, which is predominantly heterosexual, to be erased and replaced with the LGBTQIA community's respective version, which action is a betrayal. Explain why they attack religious institutions such as churches, oppose faith-based books in schools and public libraries, and defy God himself? The LGBTQIA community has gotten groups like Moms For Liberty, and people such as women's swimming champion Riley Gaines and former child star Kirk Cameron, known for his role in the sitcom *Growing Pains* starring Alan Thicke, the late father of the famous pop singer Robin Thicke, banned from speaking at public educational institutions and have gotten faith-based books banned from public libraries in favor of drag queen story hour storybooks. These people and groups have been silenced, censored, canceled, which is proof that many members of the LGBTQIA community want to erase God, religion, and anything faith based from our society and replace it with its own versions. The LGBTQIA community and everything it stands for is the leftists' religion, always putting up resistance against the heterosexual community and seeking to replace religion or acts of faith.

The reason they seek to replace the Judeo-Christian faith tradition is that they have no way to get around or past what the Bible has to say about sexuality and/or homosexuality. The Bible imposes a system of checks and balances on the LGBTQIA community by naming which behaviors are moral and which are immoral. This stops them from going rogue and trespassing on the rights of the heterosexual community to the point of the extinction of the heterosexual way of life. The LGBTQIA community wants to erase religion, the Bible, and God from every aspect of our society because these things get in their way and impose a system of checks and balances on them, which they dislike. Therefore the LGBTQIA community wants these faith-based institutions and religions to be completely banned, erased, and destroyed.

The LGBTQIA community is changing how Americans think about heterosexuality. They are also bending the rules of society in hopes of replacing them with their own versions—and their values—and using the threat of being called homophobic as a weapon and way to put fear into heterosexuals so that they come to favor the LGBTQIA community and give them an advantage over heterosexuals, which allows the LGBTQIA community to gain and then keep power. That to me is bullying, disdain, hatred, and heterophobia, along with being a betrayal of the heterosexual community. How is it not, when the LGBTQIA community gained our trust by asking only for tolerance and acceptance, and now that they are a so-called "protected class," they have turned on the heterosexual community and stabbed us in the back by becoming heterophobic and trying to erase heterosexuality from every aspect of our society? The LGBTQIA community has betrayed the heterosexual community by trying to shame us and bully us into the closet by falsely accusing us of homophobia, a so-called "offense," to elicit fear. Now in some cases the LGBTQIA community is trying to criminalize the use of gender-specific pronouns, having heterosexuals kicked out of schools or be fired from their jobs and/or put in jail if they fail to use the proper pronoun to address someone in the LGBTQIA community. The motive here is to make the language preferred by the LGBTQIA community the dominant and/or only acceptablelanguage, and not the heterosexual language, in society, thereby erasing the language used by the heterosexual community. In truth, the heterophobia of the LGBTQIA community is at the forefront here. It is what is driving the disdain, hatred, and treachery of most, not all, in the LGBTQIA community.

Another unsavory truth is that the LGBTQIA community has piggybacked on heterosexual feminist movement and the black civil rights movement and has stolen and used the pain of these groups, which struggled against discrimination, to help them advance their own cause in society. And now the LGBTQIA community, after getting what they wanted and becoming a so-called "protected class," has turned its back on these groups and has begun recruiting their children in schools and indoctrinating them with the LGBTQIA versions of men, women, and other things, promoting these versions over the heterosexual versions. Now the LGBTQIA community is trying to erase everything that these heterosexual groups stand for. And if they can't use these groups to further their own agenda, which is to take over our society, then they will turn around like a snake and bite them! This is the alphabet mob in full effect, using shaming and bullying tactics to force heterosexuals to bow down to them and bend to their will. It's a betrayal!

Some readers may say that what I claim is untrue and that the language I use to make my case is homophobic. To these readers, I ask, is the heterosexual lifestyle the same as the homosexual lifestyle? The answer is no, correct? Do homosexuals want to be forced to be more like heterosexuals? That's a no too, right? Which would the LGBTQIA community prefer, homosexuals to be more like heterosexuals, or heterosexuals to be more like homosexuals? I take it that they want heterosexuals to be more like homosexuals. Why do I say that? Because of what I see everywhere in our society everywhere. The LGBTQIA community has started a takeover campaign against heterosexuality and in favor of the LGBTQIA movement. First they start with heterosexual women. The LGBTQIA community and all the leftists do not want to recognize heterosexual women as either women or mothers. Why not? What do I mean? OK, here's what I mean: Some people on the Left have been asked, "What is a woman?" and they have all pretended not to have an answer. The Supreme Court justice Ketanji Brown Jackson, at her confirmation hearing, said that she didn't know what a woman was, even though she is a woman herself. The LGBTQIA community and other leftists call mothers "birthing people" instead of "mothers." Why? Because they want their version of a woman and a mother, not the heterosexual community's version, to be the standard. That is an instance of hate and heterophobia. It's also a betrayal. The LGBTQIA community want their version of a woman, which is a transgender woman, that is, a biological male, to predominate in sports. They want these biological males competing with biological females so that the former can dominate heterosexual women. The LGBTQIA community doesn't want to call a married couple "husband and wife." Why not? Because they want their version of a married couple, and not the heterosexual community's version, to be the standard—another instance of hate and heterophobic betrayal.

Most (not all)of the LGBTQIA community is going after every

aspect of the heterosexual community to reengineer society. That includes pop culture and big business. The LGBTQIA community wants their version of a woman and their version of language to be the standards, with the heterosexual standards erased. Again, this is an instance of betrayal, hate, and heterophobia. Now the LGBTQIA community is going after the heterosexuals' schoolchildren—further evidence of heterophobia, hate, and betrayal. I say it's betrayal because the LGBTQIA community originally lured the heterosexual community in by asking for so-called "tolerance," and then equality, and now they want to erase the heterosexual community from existence, which is heterophobia. Now that the homosexual community has gained the trust of the heterosexual community, along with their acceptance and tolerance, they have turned and stabbed the heterosexual community in the back by trying to eliminate everything having anything to do with heterosexuality and replacing it with their version. Now where does that leave the heterosexual community? SOL, meaning shit out of luck. And most, not all, members of the LGBTQIA community don't give a damn about equality for heterosexuals as long as they get what they want. That's a betrayal.

Now you may be asking why am I going after the LGBTQIA community. *If you're doing this,* you think, *then you are homophobic.* And that's the problem. Everyone and everything has to be subjected to a system of checks and balances. Who is checking the LGBTQIA community to make sure that they are honest and haven't gone too far into stealing the heterosexual community's rights? The answer is no one, and that's how they are succeeding at bullying heterosexuals, changing heterosexual standards to homosexual ones, taking over society, and erasing heterosexuality from existence.

The LGBTQIA community is not fighting a fair fight. They are fighting with fire, and tying the hands of heterosexuals behind our backs so that we can't fight back equally or fairly, and the heterosexual community is trying to put out that fire with water, remaining on the defense and trying to fight fairly, while the LGBTQIA community continues fighting dirty.

I'm exposing the unfairness and the low blows that the LGBTQIA community are dealing. Meaning, I'm fighting fire with fire. Sometimes it's necessary, and in this case it is a must because we heterosexuals are being erased from existence with most everyone too afraid to disagree with the LGBTQIA community because then the alphabet mob will come after them. Well, someone has got to stand up for the heterosexual community's rights. So if I have to go it alone, then so be it. I'm just exposing the truth and citing the facts. To anyone who doesn't like it, I say to you, "Frankly, my dear, I don't give a damn." We'll let the chips fall where they may. I'm just exposing the truth and saying what millions are afraid to say publicly. Why are they afraid to speak out against the LGBTQIA community? It's because the LGBTQIA community has gained a great deal of social power over heterosexuals, and therefore they feel emboldened and entitled to destroy the lives of heterosexuals at will with their mob-like mentality.

Now the LGBTQIA community has set its sights on targeting, trying to recruit heterosexual children and indoctrinate them with the LGBTQIA community lifestyle to get these children on the LGBTQIA side and against heterosexuals, even their own parents. How are they doing this? By keeping parents out of their own schoolchildren's permanent-life altering decisions—the perfect way to recruit, indoctrinate and subject heterosexual children to gay sexualization. Bullying parents who are supposedly homophobic is a backdoor way of keeping them at bay, which allows the LGBTQIA community to take over the parental role and to go ahead and carry out its gay indoctrination agenda, unchecked and unchallenged by parents or anyone else.

The LGBTQIA community has gone from tolerance, to equality, to heterophobia, and is now at the indoctrination stage. Schools, which are now battlegrounds for the minds and bodies of heterosexual children, are on the front lines of this culture war. The objective of this battle is to indoctrinate heterosexual children and turn them gay or into LGBTQIA community activists, who will fight for the LGBTQIA cause. To stop parents from protecting their own children, the LGBTQIA community deems them to be transphobic, bullies, and domestic terrorists. These indoctrination groups are saying things like, "No parent has the right to injure their children." They are saying that parents are injuring their own children by protecting them against sex change surgery, which is permanent! On top of this, they are saying that parents should let their underage children, who are too young to get a driver's license, purchase alcohol, or even vote, make a permanent, life-altering gender-reassignment decision all on their own and without the help, guidance, or consent of their parents. This is a sneaky, underhanded betrayal by the LGBTQIA community, seeking to turn heterosexual children into homosexual children so as to gain numbers and support for implementing their takeover agenda. And more than this, it's their way of erasing the heterosexual community from existence. Because they have a sense of entitlement over heterosexuals, being a so-called "protected class," they think they have the right, including the legal right, to bully you, attack you, and force you to bow down to them and make you concede, to your own heterosexual demise. This is how the alphabet mob operates.

The more children they can succeed in persuading to get a sex change operation, the more they will be able to indoctrinate all children. This is because our society will have fewer heterosexual children in the future if this plan should succeed. Now these children, when they become adults, will indoctrinate their children with the LGBTQIA line of thinking, and this same pattern will be repeated year after year, decade after decade, and generation after generation, until heterosexuals become nonexistent. This plan is a betrayal and a far cry from so-called "tolerance."

The LGBTQIA community is playing the long game. Back in the late eighties and early nineties, when the gay community sought to have homosexuality taught in grade school, there was a big uproar about it. The heterosexual community caved in because they didn't want to be viewed as homophobic. So you see that this type of recruitment and indoctrination has been carried out before. And here we go again—but this time it's ten times more potent and ten times more effective than before because the LGBTQIA community seeks to go directly after heterosexual children, this time without the parents' knowledge or consent. Now, who are those children from the late eighties and early nineties? They are the millennials and Gen Z'ers, the most progay and pro-LGBTQIA-community sympathizers in our nation's history. Why are they this way? Because they were targeted and indoctrinated by the LGBTQIA community, and now the community has favor with these two generations.

This time, this plan is to erase the heterosexual community as a whole and replace it with the LGBTQIA community, which will be the dominant and the most powerful group. Don't believe it? Just look at how the LGBTQIA community is replacing women in our society. They are pretending that that don't know what a woman is or how to define a woman. They are putting transgender women, that is, biological males, in sports and in locker rooms with heterosexual women, in turn erasing heterosexual women and replacing them with their own version of women: biological males. So, they have betrayed straight women, after these women accepted them and helped them gain momentum for their cause of promoting their community. Now the LGBTQIA community is erasing heterosexual women from existence. They are also betraying parents by going after their children in schools, getting at them at an early age and getting them to change their gender without their parents' knowledge or consent, thereby causing heterosexuality to become extinct. The LGBTQIA community is going after every educational institution, from grade school to college, as well as corporations, marketing agencies, advertising agencies, the military, the film industry, and the music industry. You name it, and these entities have placed the LGBTQIA stamp of approval on it, at the same time excluding anything and anyone that's heterosexual. Therefore, they have betrayed the heterosexual community. Now the LGBTQIA community is attacking heterosexual marriage. They want to call married couples "spouses" rather than "husband and wife." So why do they want to attack heterosexual marriage? It's because a gay couple who are married—either two men or two women—can't call themselves "husband and wife, because it's either two men or two women, so they want to tear down heterosexual marriage and replace it with their own version: gay marriage. The LGBTQIA community is trying to destroy the heterosexual community's way of thinking and way of life and replace it with the gay version, including the gay definitions of thinking and living. This is another betrayal of the heterosexual community. This attack by the LGBTQIA community and their heterophobia is all about transforming US society into an LGBTQIA society. This is a betrayal, their having taking things this far after asking only for our acceptance and tolerance.

The LGBTQIA community view is that if you accept some of their ideas as far as who they are, or if you accept some of them, then you have to accept all their ideas, even if you think those ideas are crazy, bad, or wrong, and even if you think they are potentially pedophilic. And you have to accept drag queen story hour for heterosexual children even if it goes against your deepest heterosexual values. It doesn't matter: it's the gay way or no way. It's the way the LGBTQIA community sees and views society today, and *not* the way that heterosexuals view things. This is the LGBTQIA community's betrayal. To further establish their social dominance is why they are going after the heterosexual lifestyle and heterosexual children by implementing drag queen story hour in schools, imposing gay sexuality curriculums in grade schools (in books and in the classroom), making puberty blockers available for minors, encouraging heterosexual minor children to have permanent sex change operations without their parents' knowledge or permission, claiming that certain kids are trans kids, advocating for biological men to compete in women's sports and be allowed in women's locker rooms, and on and on. The endgame is to recruit and/ or indoctrinate as many heterosexual children as possible and erase the heterosexual community from existence so as to replace it with LGBTQIA community. Hence, the betrayal of heterosexuals after we granted the LGBTQIA community tolerance and acceptance, which was the gateway to their deception and the erosion of our children and our society. The so-called "tolerance and acceptance" the LGBTQIA community asked for turned out to be a Trojan horse, a thing to cause the heterosexual community to let down our guard so that the LGBTQIA community could then destroy us from within.

The LGBTQIA community can't be trusted! Look at what our trust in them got us! Women have been erased in women's sports and are being replaced by biological males, something the LGBTQIA community fought very hard to accomplish, and our children being indoctrinated by drag queens and teachers (who could be potential pedophiles) reading from homosexual books. I say potential because we don't know who is talking our young, innocent children and teaching them about sex, because these LGBTQIA educators have told the children to keep such sexual secrets to themselves and not tell their parents. How creepy is that? Now that's what our trust in the LGBTQIA community has gotten us. Which is betrayed. And now the LGBTQIA community has waged a war on words. Why? Because whoever controls the language is able to control the people and get the outcome they want. And in this instance, the outcome is destruction of the heterosexual lifestyle. Once the LGBTQIA community controls the language, they can replace whatever they wish with their own terms and expressions, in so doing taking over American society. Then they'll be able to run the country after having scared the heterosexual community into the closet and caused heterosexuals to become extinct. Hence, the betrayal.

Heterosexuals, you must take a stand against this betrayal if you want to maintain your lifestyle, mindset, faith, religious freedom, and freedom of speech. The LGBTQIA community is at war with the heterosexual community over who gets to control US society. Heterosexuals, don't be terribly concerned about offending the LGBTQIA community. Accusing you of homophobia is their trump card and their cue to send the alphabet mob out to silence you and censor your voice so as to weaken your ability to oppose them and their outrageous behavior and conduct, thereby keeping you at bay and dividing you from your children, whom they want to recruit, indoctrinate, and turn either gay or into LGBTQIA activists—that is, turn your own children against you. Taking away your freedom of speech is the first step toward controlling you as a heterosexual and controlling US society and the country as a whole. Again, this is a betrayal. Heterosexuals, take a stand or else be erased. I know that the LGBTQIA community is going to say that my language is offensive. If so, it would be typical of how they act in order to silence anyone who doesn't agree with them or support their agenda to betray the heterosexual community, erase heterosexuals from society, and take over. By exposing the betrayal of the LGBTQIA community, I'm taking a stand.

The LGBTQIA community uses three tactics, namely, the offensiveness seeker, the emotional keeper, and the sympathetic bully—terms that I have devised—to try to silence, censor, and destroy anyone who gets in the way of its agenda. What is an emotional keeper? This is a person who can't measure up or compete on an equal playing field with those who are mentally and emotionally tougher, stronger, and more confident than they are. These kind of people intentionally lower their emotions and tolerance level to zero because they can't handle any opposition, when everyone else in society has to raise their tolerance level in order to handle the opposing person's viewpoint, whom they don't agree with or like. Therefore, by intentionally weakening themselves so that they become unable to handle anything, and by claiming that everything is offensive to them, those among the LGBTQIA community get everyone else to take responsibility for their emotions, ensuring that their feelings don't hurt, while these individuals do absolutely nothing to strengthen themselves. In this way, they gain control of everyone around them. It's a con game they're playing. That's why therapy, psychiatry, and medication are available. But instead of getting help to improve their weaknesses, the members of the LGBTQIA community tear down and try to control the stronger, more confident, and more capable people because they can't measure up to them.

Now what is a sympathetic bully? A sympathy bully is someone who intentionally plays the victim in order to get other people around them to fight their fights and their battles for them, with the sympathetic bully getting these people to attack, shame, silence, censor, destroy, and bully the person whose behavior toward them they deemed to be offensive. By playing the victim, the sympathetic bully gets sympathy and support from those around them. But at the same time, they get others to turn into a mob and attack the people who oppose them. This is a very effective tactic used by many, but not all, in the LGBTQIA community. By using the tactic of emotional keeper and sympathetic bully is how the LGBTQIA community is silencing, censoring, destroying, and betraying the heterosexual community.

Heterosexuals, you had better take a stand or become extinct. The LGBTQIA community has betrayed the heterosexual community by intentionally becoming a so-called "protected class" and then immediately setting about bullying the heterosexual community at will and making them bow down to them and comply with anything that they want, Including indoctrinating heterosexual children and transforming them into homosexual children without their parents' knowledge or consent. The LGBTQIA community believes that they are in charge now and that the heterosexual community had better do as they say, or else they will be shamed, silenced, censored, and destroyed by the alphabet mob. That's the betrayal. The LGBTQIA community can no longer be trusted. They have taken our kindness, acceptance, and tolerance for weakness, while they try to destroy heterosexual women, children, the heterosexual lifestyle, and society as a whole, at the same time replacing these things with their own versions, forcing heterosexuals into the closet, and demanding that heterosexual comply with their new world order. Heterosexuals, take a stand now. The LGBTQIA community is at war with you over the right to live your life as you choose, your right to freedom of speech, and control over your children.

If you don't believe this, then take a look at so-called gender-affirming or gender-transition care. Congress held a hearing on July 27, 2023, on this very issue. A young woman named Chloe Cole testified on the congressional floor and told her story of how doctors had coerced her parents into accepting her for who she is as a person. This is what the doctors asked her parents: "Would you rather have a dead daughter or a living transgender boy?" Chloe said she "felt like a monster" after the transition. Remember that puberty-blocking drugs are experimental and that minor children who making permanent life-altering decisions all on their own because the schools and the doctors are excluding the parents and depriving them of any knowledge or warnings about their own children, along with refusing to ask for their permission for serious procedures affecting their own children.

So why is the LGBTQIA community, along with doctors, lawmakers, and the schools, doing this? For the doctors, it's about the money. Yes, the almighty dollar. This new transgender care is a multibillion-dollar business. For the LGBTQIA community, it's about erasing the heterosexual community from existence and getting people who are more favorable toward the LGBTQIA community to become activists and further their cause and agenda, that is, replacing the heterosexual version of gender and lifestyle with the LGBTQIA version of gender and lifestyle. For the lawmakers, it's about the votes to keep them in power. And for the schools, which is the gateway for all the others, it's about gay pedophiles having access to young, innocent heterosexual children, whom the LGBTQIA community doesn't give a damn about. If they did, then they would let the parents make the decisions for their own children, whom they are responsible for. But they don't. To the LGBTQIA community, the schools, the doctors, and the politicians, your heterosexual children are just collateral damage. Just ask young people like Chloe Cole, who went through the pain of gender reassignment surgery without her parents' knowledge or permission.

Heterosexuals, it's time to take a stand. To hell with "offending" the LGBTQIA community when they have betrayed your trust and are trying to erase you from existence. Now I'm not say saying get physical, because there is no place for violence, which is wrong no matter which side you're on, but I am saying to stand up for your rights, voice your opinions, and stop the LGBTQIA community from recruiting and indoctrinating your children. Remember, physical abuse has no place in our society, but speaking your mind and standing up for yourself does. It's the American way. We as a society can no longer be concerned about people's feelings when many (not all) in the LGBTQIA community are trying to destroy us as a gender. We have been betrayed by many (not all) in the LGBTQIA community, and it's time to take a stand. We who are part of the heterosexual community have let our guard down and accepted the LGBTQIA community, many of whom hate our lifestyle and what we stand for. These people are hell-bent on destroying the heterosexual lifestyle by any means necessary, including indoctrination of minor children and erasing heterosexuality from the earth. The leaders of the LGBTQIA community have threatened parents and told them that they will lose custody if they don't allow their minor children to undergo an experimental permanent gender-altering surgery and that it's their undeveloped minor child who will have the last word on this issue—the same minor child who is too young to vote, purchase alcohol, buy a gun to defend himself or herself, and drive a car. Such threats are mob-like tactics, and in some instances it's coercion. Read chapter 5 for more on the alphabet mob's Mafia-style tactics. I call them the alphabet mob because they use coercion tactics just like the Mafia. This is only one example of such mob tactics.

Now many (not all) in the LGBTQIA community have betrayed the church and mocked people of faith and their religion, and no one from the LGBTQIA community has stood up to condemn this offensive group. They are an offensive group of drag queens called the "Sisters of Perpetual Indulgence." This gay group performs strip tease shows at clubs dressed up as Catholic nuns on the cross, mocking Jesus Christ and people of faith. The show is lewd and disgusting, and most members (not all) of the LGBTQIA community condone this betrayal of the Christian faith by their silence. And this is yet another attack on heterosexuality by many (not all) in the LGBTQIA community. Why do I say this? Because the Sisters of Perpetual Indulgence and the LGBTQIA community as a whole know that they have to destroy the image of the Christian faith, and the religion as a whole, and the standard of morality that it holds us all to if they are to have permission to commit their immoral acts. This way they replace the Bible and Christianity, substituting them with their own agenda and their own faith. They do this because it is the LGBTQIA community's equivalent of religion.

The LGBTQIA movement is the faith of those on the Left! The LGBTQIA community wants to replace God and established religious faiths with their own leftist faith, which involves the gay lifestyle. Have you noticed that every time the Christian faith is discussed on TV, the network has someone from the LGBTQIA community to appear to counter that religion? It's no mere coincidence as to why most (not all) in the LGBTQIA community is attacking heterosexuals' religion. The LGBTQIA community betrays the heterosexual community at every turn and in every area that matters to heterosexuals.

Heterosexuals had better take a stand now! The LGBTQIA community is trying to erase our God and religious beliefs and replace these with their own perverted version of religion, like the Sisters of Perpetual Indulgence, which group is part of the LGBTQIA religion. The LGBTQIA community has plotted a takeover of our society right in front of our eyes, replacing our society with their version in every area in our society an trying to force us to live by their beliefs and rules, by indoctrinating us or bullying us into the closet. Take a stand, heterosexuals: you are being attacked, and your trust has been betrayed! Heterosexuals, you must love your innocent children more than you allow yourself to worry about what is supposedly offensive to someone else, especially when offensiveness is used against you in order to bully you into the closet or erase your heterosexuality.

Chapter 2

What Is Heterophobia?

Tyranny of the minority is a culture of oppression and harsh and unjust acts.

The LGBTQIA community does not get to ram their identity or ideology down our throats and bully heterosexuals into the closet. We get to decide our own identity and beliefs.

Heterophobes are members of the LGBTQIA community who dislike or hate heterosexuals or the straight/heterosexual lifestyle. They want to attack the heterosexual lifestyle, destroy it, and replace it with the LGBTQIA lifestyle.

Heterosexuals do not have a monopoly on hate. Many (not all) in LGBTQIA community have proven that they can discriminate and be just as hateful as heterosexuals. This hate is disguised as, or put under the umbrella of, tolerance, equality, and DEI (diversity, equity, and inclusion). Also, the "sympathetic bully," the "emotional keeper," and the manufacture of homophobic outrage help disguise the hate present among some members of the LGBTQIA community.

We have laws and rules in place, such as hate crime laws, to deal with homophobic acts and hateful people who attack members of the LGBTQIA community. However, heterophobia is also very real, as there are many among the LGBTQIA community who scream, yell, cancel, discriminate, and spread their disrespectful hate onto the heterosexual community because they believe that they are entitled given their protected class status, which the heterosexual community does not have.

So certain members of the LGBTQIA community hate at will and get away with it, suffering no consequences for their actions. Why? Because they can always claim they are victims of homophobia when they get into an altercation with a heterosexual person, even though they are the ones who started acting or speaking hatefully. Example: the LGBTQIA community will send some of their members out to oppose individuals like Riley Gaines, a female swimmer, in order to physically block them from entering certain sports arenas and also violently protest and assault them. That's what happened at a ceremonial bill signing in Texas. Members of the LGBTQIA community were throwing water and spitting on Riley Gaines and the other attendees, which is assault, and no police or other authorities were called to help these *victims* of violence and assault perpetrated by these members of the LGBTQIA community. If the situation were reversed? The people committing violent acts would have been charged with a hate crime. However, there are no laws in place to protect heterosexuals from LGBTQIA members committing hate crimes against them, bullying them, or vicious attacking them.

That's why heterophobia has picked up steam, having spread like wildfire and crossed the line, lighting into heterosexual rights. Just like a rose is still a rose by any other name, hate is still hate no matter what group practices it. The alphabet mob was manufactured— invented and created—because there are no laws protecting heterosexuals from homosexual attacks. This is not random, it was by design. It was planned to stamp out heterosexuality and replace it with homosexuality, thereby giving the LGBTQIA community power over heterosexuals. And that's just what you see in today's society: a homosexual takeover of the heterosexual power structure.

Heterosexuals, this is why you feel that today's society is unfair. The LGBTQIA community can attack you at will with no restrictions on them, but you can't respond to their attacks. Why not? It's because they have tied your hands behind your back by deeming everything homophobic, which is really manufactured outrage on their part, which they do so they can claim to be a victim of homophobia, when in reality it's just you as a heterosexual pushing back and trying to take back your right to freedom of speech, because you are under vicious verbal attack by the alphabet mob, that is, the LGBTQIA community. When many (not all) in the LGBTQIA community label everything that they dislike or disagree with, saying it is homophobia, they are literally taking your rights away from you with their heterophobia. We all, not just the LGBTQIA community, have a right to say what we choose because of the First Amendment. You may not like or may simply disagree with someone else's opinion, but that person still has the right to speak it. Otherwise, it would be censorship and heterophobia. When someone from the LGBTQIA community says that someone shouldn't be "allowed" to say something, they are displaying heterophobia. Who are they to tell someone what they are allowed to say? That just shows you the sense of entitlement that those in the LGBTQIA community have, believing themselves to be first before heterosexuals. That's taking away and/or "erasing" the heterosexual voice so that the voices of those among the LGBTQIA community are the only ones heard. That's a betrayal.

Now let's reverse the scenario. Let a heterosexual person say that the LGBTQIA community should be silenced and that their voices shouldn't be allowed to be heard. I'm quite sure that the LGBTQIA community would call that homophobia. So what's the difference?

There is no difference. It's just that the LGBTQIA community believes that they are entitled over the heterosexual community. But they're wrong. The heterosexual community has to push back and take a stand because their rights are being taking away from them by the LGBTQIA community, which is heterophobia and a betrayal.

The LGBTQIA or homosexual community has gained strength and power over the past few years of the Biden administration, and some of that power has been used to steamroll heterosexuality into extinction. You may be thinking right now that we have a duty to protect the LGBTQIA community from hate crimes and discrimination. That may be so. But this protected class of people has lost track of reality to the point where they believe that nobody can disagree with, question, debate with, or oppose them, or call them out on their wrongdoing, because they believe that any opposition to them is a hate crime or homophobia even if it is not. So now, with a taste of unchecked and unchallenged power, they have swayed the lawmakers and have taken heterosexuals' rights to use in their own favor. Society has overcorrected for the lack of rights for the LGBTQIA community in the past, and now it is time to rein the laws back in and make things equal and fair for heterosexuals again.

From this so-called "protected class" have come discrimination against and hate for heterosexuals, to the point where straight people are being bullied as now the LGBTQIA community is trying to bully heterosexuals into the closet and make heterosexuality extinct. What do I mean by extinction? There is a hidden agenda put forth by the LGBTQIA community to erase women from existence, from politicians to Supreme Court justices, for example, Ketanji Brown Jackson, who pretended that she couldn't define a woman. Now why does something so obvious go unacknowledged by the leftist LGBTQIA community and some of the most powerful Democrats in the country? It's because they want to replace the heterosexual female with the LGBTQIA version of a female, which is a transgender female, a.k.a. a biological male. By blurring the lines, the trans female can gain power in society and eventually erase the heterosexual females. The LGBTQIA community's agenda is to take over the power structure, replacing the heterosexual community. This is one way that they are doing it, by refusing to acknowledge heterosexual women. This is to erase heterosexual women from every area of society and replace them with the LGBTQIA version of a woman, which is a biological male who says that he is a woman. However, he still has a penis and testosterone, so calling himself a woman is just playing a name game, not biology.

This strategy has worked in sports. Let's take a look at trans women who are defeating biological women in track and field and swimming. Biological males who refer to themselves as transgender women are destroying women's sports to the point where women have become obsolete and irrelevant. According to the LGBTQIA community, a biological woman is unnecessary when we can have a trans woman, which is their version of a woman. Now they want to pretend that a man can get pregnant. How on earth can a man get pregnant? This is yet another example of the LGBTQIA community's erasing biological women from the face of the earth. Why are they doing this? Because biological women and feminists have a lot of power in this country, and the LGBTQIA community is competing with them for that power. There can be only one queen bee, and according to the LGBTQIA community, that queen is going to be a drag queen. The LGBTQIA community has used straight women and the feminist movement to help them further their cause against straight males and male dominance by joining together or teaming up against straight men to take them out of power. Now that the LGBTQIA community has gained power with its protected class status, its members have thrown feminists and all women under the bus because they no longer have any use for biological women, because biological women represent what the dominant straight man used to be, which is control. So, biological women must be destroyed and wiped out of existence. This is the only way the LGBTQIA community can maintain their power over our society, by eliminating the competition, as heterosexual women are the new enemy. Women's groups were deceived and/or tricked into supporting the LGBTQIA community, who pretended that they were on the same side as heterosexual women against the heterosexual men who dominated and controlled them. However, that ended up being a Trojan horse. The hidden agenda of the LGBTQIA community was to use heterosexual women, take control, and then discard them like trash along with the men.

Don't believe me? Then ask yourself why gay women's soccer star Megan Rapinoe and other powerful gay stars and politicians won't support biological women in their quest to remove biological gay or trans men athletes from women sports. I'll tell you why. Because the LGBTQIA community was never on the women's side to begin with. They have as much dislike of straight women as they have of straight men. They deceitfully aligned themselves with heterosexual women, driven by their underlying heterophobia—a betrayal. It was always about the LGBTQIA community being accepted and gaining power. Now that they have power through their protected class status, it's time for them to use it to take over the country. For this to happen, everyone and everything heterosexual has to be destroyed and replaced by versions chosen by the LGBTQIA community or homosexuals. Don't believe it? Then explain why many (not all) in the LGBTQIA community want their pronouns changed from *he* and *him* or *she* and *her* to *they* and *them*? They don't want to be a part of anything that has to do with heterosexuality, and *he* and *she* represents heterosexuality and not homosexuality. Also explain why members of the LGBTQIA community want nonbinary names. Explain why they don't want to define what a woman is. Explain why they are putting transgender people in positions traditionally occupied by biological males and biological females, replacing them. Explain why members of the LGBTQIA community are going in to grade schools to teach heterosexual children as young as first grade, who don't even know what a penis or vagina is yet, about transgender or homosexual sex. The motive is to erase heterosexuality and replace it with homosexuality. I know that you see this underlying agenda everywhere in today's society. If anyone doesn't agree with them, then they will call that person homophobic in order to silence, censor, and cancel his or her voice or opinion so that it is irrelevant and can't be heard, so that the alphabet mob can complete the LGBTQIA takeover of society. However, the endgame is to make heterosexuality nonexistent. By blurring the lines and gaslighting everyone into believing that they don't know what a woman is and calling everyone homophobic who doesn't agree with them, the LGBTQIA community is going through the back door to your children's schools and through the front door of major corporations to further their agenda of erasing heterosexuality into extinction.

The LGBTQIA community has tied heterosexuals' hands behind their backs by getting them to join them and celebrate their cause. And if anyone doesn't want to celebrate the LGBTQIA community with them, then the individual will be called homophobic, then canceled and destroyed. Do you see a pattern here?

This hateful bullying tactic is the way that the LGBTQIA community has obtained and now maintains power and control over the heterosexual community, at the same time trying to destroy it.

What makes the LGBTQIA community think that they can't be criticized or scrutinized if they do wrong? Who gave them the power to believe that they are above reproach? They are equal to heterosexuals in every way, and also includes negative ways. Accountability is a must on both sides. There must be checks and balances on both sides. I ask a question: who is checking and balancing out the LGBTQIA community and stopping them from hating and discriminating against heterosexuals? It seems that no one can say or do anything to challenge or question them without being accused of homophobia. The answer to my question is no one. So the LGBTQIA community has gone unchallenged and been allowed to go unchecked to carry out its agenda of erasing heterosexuality, recruiting and indoctrinating schoolchildren, and bullying heterosexuals into the closet. You may be wondering, where is the fairness for heterosexual? This is your answer: there is no fairness for heterosexuals if most (not all) in the LGBTQIA community has any say in the matter. Heterosexuals, you had better wake up before it's too late and before you are erased into extinction.

If you think that I'm attacking the LGBTQIA community, then allow me to ask you a question. How would you feel if heterosexuals were unchallenged and allowed to go unchecked, tearing you down and erasing homosexuality out of existence? Oh right, they were at one time, and you fought like hell to get your rights and to stop the hate and discrimination that was inflicted upon you. So now why do you believe that you can hate, discriminate, and fail to acknowledge a simple fact like what a woman is. You want to bully people into calling you *they* or *them* rather than *he* and *him* or *she* and *her*, which is a double standard and hypocritical. On the other side of the coin, you want to call people homophobic and cancel them if you don't get your way. This is infringement on the right to freedom of speech for heterosexuals. So you, the LGBTQIA community, don't have the right to look upon yourself as a so-called "victim" when you are victimizing others by not acknowledging what a woman is and gaslighting people by saying that you don't know what one is or refusing to say it.

Let me give you an example of the double standards and hypocrisy of the LGBTQIA community. I have personally seen gay men and gay women sexually harass straight or heterosexual men and women because they felt entitled, believing that any criticism of them would be considered homophobic. When heterosexuals defend themselves against unwanted attention or attacks from members of the LGBTQIA community, the gay persons turns it around and calls the heterosexuals homophobic, trying to get them charged with a hate crime or fired from their jobs even though they were the victims of sexual harassment by the gay person. This just shows that many (not all) members of the LGBTQIA community believe that because they are a protected class, they are entitled and can do no wrong, because they are the only ones who are allowed to be so-called "victims" of a hate crime. They think that they own victimhood, which makes them immune from criticism or scrutiny and indemnifies them against being hateful toward other groups, especially heterosexuals. Many LGBTQIA members consider this payback, even when they are clearly in the wrong. Equality has to be promoted on both sides and not be reserved solely for the so-called "protected class." Everyone should be a protected class, not just LGBTQIA community members. If members of the LGBTQIA community believe that they should get special privileges because they are homosexual, then they have a false sense of entitlement, and which will only reinforce my point that they want to erase heterosexuality and take away the rights of heterosexuals. Why? Because they are biased and they want power over heterosexuals to be able to hold them accountable for their wrongdoings. But they don't want the LGBTQIA community to be held accountable for their negative behavior or actions and wrongdoing.

Heterophobia is real, and it's being used by many (not all) in the LGBTQIA community to hate and discriminate against heterosexuals, take away our freedom of speech, prevent us from voicing our opinions, and push us into the closet and locking the door behind us. We as a nation have overcorrected in favor of the LGBTQIA community to the point where they have gone too far in terms of wanting to curtail heterosexual rights. It's time to push back and take our freedom and rights back, because most (not all) LGBTQIA members want to have us heterosexuals erased. To this day, I haven't heard one leftist politician come out and condemn the behavior of transgender women, that is, biological males, nor have I heard anyone challenge the LGBTQIA community on the erasing of women. That's interesting, and it proves my point that the LGBTQIA community is seeking to erase heterosexuality and cause it to become extinct. Some readers likely are going to call me homophobic to try to tear me down or cancel me, or try to have me punished in some way. There is a saying, "If you don't like the message, then attack the messenger." If any LGBTQIA reader attacks me (the messenger), then he or she would be only proving my point that the LGBTQIA community will try to cancel and destroy anyone who challenges, disagrees with, opposes, or debates the LGBTQIA community. It would also proves my point that the LGBTQIA community feels entitled and beyond reproach, even if someone points out the hypocrisy and the double standard. The LGBTQIA community wants total annihilation and extinction of heterosexuality, with its biases, double standards, and lack of accountability. However, I'm pushing back. No one has pointed out these double standards and biases because they are too afraid of the backlash from the alphabet mob. Right is right and wrong is wrong, and I'm not scared of the alphabet mob or the sympathetic bully, because I'm speaking the truth—and the truth shall set you free. What the LGBTQIA community is displaying is heterophobia in full effect.

Chapter 3

Beware of the LGBTQIA Deception: The "Sympathetic Bully," The "Emotional Keeper," The "Offensiveness Seeker," and Manufactured Outrage

Members of the LGBTQIA community don't want men or women to defend their own manhood or womanhood. They want to be able to tear it down at will with no opposition against them and with no defense or protection for heterosexuals. The key for heterosexuals is not to allow the weak and underachievers to make you feel guilty as if you have done them wrong. If they can't measure up, that is their problem, not yours. As for me, I will leave them with the problem because I don't owe them anything!

What the LGBTQIA community is doing amounts to gender assassination tactic and a plot to destroy all things heterosexual.

Tyranny of the minority—a culture of oppression, harsh and unjust acts.

The LGBTQIA community does not get to ram their identity or

ideology down our throats and bully heterosexuals into the closet. We get to decide our own identity and beliefs.

What Is a Victim Mentality?

A victim mentality is an acquired personality trait where a person tends to recognize or consider himself or herself as a so-called "victim" of the negative actions of others, and then behaves as if such were the case in the face of any contrary evidence.

What Is a Sympathetic Bully?

This is an LGBTQIA member who, through "sympathy," gets others to feel sorry for him or her and make it appear as if a big, strong, confident man or woman is beating up on this poor, defenseless LGBTQIA member or "victim." The objective is to instill a mob-like mentality in as many gay and heterosexual women and men as possible and get them to gang up on and bully someone who opposes them, or just disagrees with them, in order to silence and censor that individual's voice so that he or she can't get his or her point across and outline whatever it is he or she wants in that situation. Then the members of LGBTQIA community win, thereby defeating all heterosexuals, not physically, but through "sympathy," that is, being a sympathetic bully.

The one thing that the LGBTQIA community can't compete with is a strong, confident alpha male–alpha female combination. So, they want to destroy these heterosexual alphas by any means necessary, along with images of everything that complements heterosexual culture. It's part of the heterosexual gender assassination plot, an effort to destroy all things heterosexual.

What Is an Offensiveness Seeker?

The offensiveness seeker is a person who goes around intentionally looking to be offended by someone or something in order to make himself or herself out to be a victim so that he or she can get sympathy from other people and then turn himself or herself into the sympathetic bully. Why would a person do that? To feel important, as this gives an LGBTQIA person some kind of significance in his or her life, because he or she doesn't have any. Offensiveness seekers are people who have no life and nothing that makes them feel important. So, by manufacturing outrage and becoming a so-called "victim," they can get attention and gain the power to bring down their opponents and the strong, confident people they can't measure up to. These are people who intentionally, manipulatively misinterpret what you are saying in order to make themselves out to be victims. Why? Because they are seekers of power and control, hoping to gain power over people they can't measure up to. They personally feel inferior to strong, confident people. They have an inferiority complex. So, they hate people who are better than they are—in any way, shape, or form.

It's like the beta male who hates the alpha male because the alpha males gets all the women's attention. So, the beta male wants to bring the alpha male down, place him beneath him, and make him look bad to the women he is unable to attract, in order to make him (the beta) feel superior.

The same is true of a beta woman.

An offensiveness-seeking woman wants to bring a strong, confident alpha male down because she can't measure up to his strength as a man. She purposely seeks to be offended by him in order to bring him down and make him bow down to her by playing the victim. Now she can become the sympathetic bully who gets others to bully this man in order to silence him, censor his voice, and make him inferior to her! She also now gets him to cater to her needs and wants.

The LGBTQIA community is no different. Many, but not all, LGBTQIA people purposely go around seeking out something or someone heterosexual to be offended by. Why? Because they feel inferior, and the way to overcome that feeling of inferiority is to intentionally turn themselves into so-called "victims" of homophobia so that it appears as if they are being bullied by heterosexuals, thereby making heterosexuals feel guilty about their situation, which enables the heterosexuals to be turned in to their emotional keepers.

This means that the emotional keeper makes everyone else responsible for his or her emotions and feelings, while he or she does absolutely nothing to raise his or her own tolerance level, like the rest of us in society. Therefore, the person can bully heterosexuals into catering to his or her needs.

These people have to be called out and exposed for what they are—bullies! These types of people are opportunists, and this is their way of gaining confidence, significance, and a sense of importance in their lives that they lack because they have an inferiority complex. Therefore, they go around seeking out people who are above them and better than them, and whom they can't measure up to, in order to bully them, silence them, censor them, make them bow down, and bring them to their knees, begging the offensiveness seeker for forgiveness for making him or her feel bad. And that is what makes the individual a sympathetic bully. Members of the LGBTQIA community do such a thing purposefully and intentionally because they are on an ego trip and this raises their self-esteem. Remember, they lack confidence and have an inferiority complex. So, beware of the offensiveness seekers.

LGBTQIA and Manufacturing Outrage

Many (not all) in the LGBTQIA community manufacture outrage in order to stop heterosexuals in their tracks from defending their own manhood or womanhood or heterosexuality. Why? Because the LGBTQIA community knows that they can't compete with heterosexuals on this level, so the plan is to stifle us. An accusation that goes unchallenged is considered to be true, so the LGBTQIA community wants only their voices heard. That way, there is only one voice (LGBTQIA) voice, one fact, and one truth, meaning that the LGBTQIA group is right and that heterosexual groups are wrong. It's deceitful manipulation, a con game. The LGBTQIA community is in control of the narrative. That way, they get their side of the story told and the heterosexuals do not. Therefore, it appears as if they are right and that the heterosexuals are wrong on the issues or topics, because there is no other option or opposing opinion or point of view out there to counter theirs. They get the last word and final say-so because they silence heterosexuals through the "sympathetic bully" tactic.

Chapter 4

LGBTQIA—Intentionally Sexualizing Heterosexual Children by Way of a Homosexual Curriculum

LGBTQIA+ Teachers in Grade Schools Are Keeping "Sexual Secrets" between Parents and Students

No Parental Oversight

A Pedophiles Dream Job

Turning Grade Schools into LGBTQIA'S Recruitment and Indoctrination Camps

The Perfect'Captive Audience'

LGBTQIA teachers in grade schools are keeping sexual secrets from the parents of their students. This is done in classrooms with no parental oversight. Therefore, teaching is now a pedophile's dream job. Grade schools are turning into LGBTQIA recruitment and indoctrination camps as schoolchildren are the perfect captive audience.

Why do schools and other educational institutions make the

best recruitment and indoctrination camps? Because the teachers or instructors have a captive audience who trusts them. The children are young, undeveloped, impressionable, and naive, there to learn, but more important, unable to question the authority figures. They believe that the schools are looking out for their best interests, but the very people who are teaching them are, in this case, brainwashing them. The instructors have unchecked authority to preach their agenda rather than teach. They impart whatever they want the children to know without any questions or pushback from students, parents, principals, or deans.

This means that no one is there to put a check on the teachers or professors to make sure that they are doing the right thing, behaving properly, and not passing propaganda onto their students. Many underage students have captured video of teachers and instructors saying or doing inappropriate things in the classroom with a captive audience, including reading from LGBTQIA books that are unauthorized and used as indoctrination tools. This borders on pedophiliac behavior, and this is why we need checks and balances in the classrooms. Some (not all) in the LGBTQIA community are crossing the line with heterosexual children and sneaking in their own viewpoints, and not the school's, in order to shape the minds of young, innocent children so they go against their parents' heterosexual values and beliefs and side with the LGBTQIA community (and against the heterosexual community). This is the deceptive way in which some members (not all) in the LGBTQIA community are using a sexual curriculum to get young children to change their gender, use puberty blockers, and make permanent life-altering sex-change decisions without their parents' knowledge or permission. This is a betrayal of parents and the erasing of the heterosexual community. The more young children that the

LGBTQIA community can indoctrinate through the schools, the fewer heterosexual adults there will be in future generations. And if any parents or adults oppose or disagree with the LGBTQIA agenda, then they will be deemed as homophobic, then be silenced, censored, and bullied into the closet by the alphabet mob. It's a war on parents and the erasing of heterosexuality by way of a sexualized curriculum. Schools are the pathway to the shaping of the young, impressionable minds of undeveloped children.

The LGBTQIA community understands this, and that's why they are targeting the schools. They seek to beat nature to the punch and get to the children first, shaping their minds into how they want them to be and not how the heterosexual parents want their children to develop. This is why the LGBTQIA community doesn't want the parents' input, involvement, or interference in the classroom, so they can have schoolchildren keeping secrets from their own parents while they are in school.

There is a famous case from August 2021 in the Loudoun County School District, in Virginia, where a father, Scott Thomas Smith, went to confront the school board about his young daughter, who was sexually assaulted in the girls' bathroom. The father wanted to address the school board members and ask them why a boy who identified as a transgender female was allowed into the girls' bathroom. This *boy*, who deceptively identify as a girl, had raped Smith's daughter, and he wanted answers. Smith had found out that the school board members and superintendent had known about the rape of his daughter and had only transferred the boy to another school in order to keep the matter quiet, rather than call the police and have the boy arrested for the sexual assault of Smith's daughter. However this boy, after being transferred, sexually assaulted another girl at the new school. Again, the LGBTQIA community didn't condemn this behavior. They were more interested in protecting the LGBTQIA community, protecting transgender bathrooms, and ensuring that they themselves did not look bad than in seeking justice for Scott Smith's daughter.

Well, instead of getting answers at the school board meeting, Smith was arrested for obstruction of justice and disorderly conduct, which he engaged in because the school board refused to let him talk about his daughter's rape. The school board members told the police, who were already there, to remove Smith because they didn't want the rest of the parents and the media to know what this so-called transgender female had done. They did this because they were pushing for a law that would allow transgender females, that is, biological males, to use the same restrooms and locker rooms in the school as girls. In essence, they were responsible for this tragedy because it was their policies that caused this assault. It's unbelievable that this grieving father was treated this way by the school board members, who covered up this crime for the LGBTQIA community.

On September 10, 2023, the new Republican governor of Virginia, Glenn Youngkin, who ran on parental rights in schools, who had won the election in 2022, pardoned the victim's father, Mr. Scott Smith. Also, the superintendent was fired and criminal charges were filed against him. However, for the heterosexual community, this incident still marks a betrayal. It also shows us how we are going to be treated by the LGBTQIA community if we don't take a stand. We can no longer be considerate of their feelings and worry being offensive toward the LGBTQIA community when they are protected from the consequences of criminal actions against heterosexuals. No one from the LGBTQIA community came out and condemned this vicious behavior by one of their members. They were more concerned about protecting gay predators and erasing heterosexuality than they were about extending compassion to anyone in the heterosexual community.

The LGBTQIA community is planning a plotted takeover of American society, which is a betrayal of the heterosexual community. If you want to erase heterosexuality from society, then schools are the perfect place to start, as there you can recruit and indoctrinate the next generations of nonbinary people, that is, LGBTQIA activists and sympathizers. By the time today's children make it through grade school, middle school, high school, and then college, heterophobia will be set as if in cement and deeply ingrained into those students' brains and mindset. At that point, the students themselves will be the ones who want to erase heterosexuality from our society. Why? Because they will only view through the homosexual lens, which is exactly the way it was planned, plotted, and executed by the LGBTQIA community. It's a betrayal of parents and of the heterosexual community's trust, achieved by way of a homosexual curriculum. It's an elaborate plot to take down and destroy heterosexuality by pulling it out by its roots. The LGBTQIA community is grooming the next generation of LGBTQIA members, rooted in heterophobia in every way, seeking the rise and empowerment of the LGBTQIA community and seeking that the LGBTQIA voice be the only voice that everyone has to listen to, thanks to the instilling of the of being canceled or destroyed and shoved into the closet. It's just the way it was designed. This is how the LGBTQIA community keeps heterosexuals at bay, while trying to destroy them and erase them at the same time.

Heterosexuals have to start pushing back and stop fearing backlash from the alphabet mob. Why? Because they are coming after you and your children anyway, whether you agree with them or not, whether you appease them or not, and whether you march with them in the pride parade or not. Therefore, you are damned if you do and damned if you don't. You are going to be shamed, intimidated, insulted, bullied, called homophobic, and attacked by the alphabet mob anyway because they have an agenda, one rooted in betrayal, and the objective is the destroy heterosexuality, erase it from our society, and punish anyone who doesn't agree with their agenda, forcing such individuals into the closet. The message is: stay silent and don't voice your opinion, even if it's your own children's future at stake. The best way to gain control of children is to sexualize the curriculum in grade schools all the way to colleges. You may as well push back for the sake of your children. That's the plan of the LGBTQIA community: to destroy heterosexuality and erase it from existence. I say to push back with the truth and the facts and let the chips fall where they may. If you don't, then those same chips are going to fall on your head. Because the schools and your heterosexual children are the target audience of the LGBTQIA community, and you will pay the price in the future for not pushing back. And unfortunately, the erasure of your identity as a heterosexual will be done by your own indoctrinated children.

Chapter 5

LGBTQIA: The Alphabet Mob Attackers-Street Gang Style Mob Attackers- Mafia Style Coercion, Extortion, Acts of Racketeering Count# Dealing in Obscene Matters

The alphabet mob attacks using street gang style. The LGBTQIA community uses mob tactics, Mafia style, including coercion, extortion, and acts of racketeering, the main count being dealing in obscene matter.

Tyranny of the minority—a culture of oppression and harsh and unjust acts.

The LGBTQIA community does not get to ram their identity or ideology down our throats and bully heterosexuals into the closet. We get to decide our own identity and beliefs.

Why do I call the LGBTQIA members the "alphabet mob"? It's for two reasons. First, because "LGBTQIA" is an initialism to which letters of the alphabet keep being added in order to strengthen the LGBTQIA numbers for purposes intimidating and bullying politicians and heterosexuals. It's like a street gang style mentality, that is, a mob of people who go out and attack individuals who disagree with them as a group. The second reason is because the LGBTQIA community at times behaves like the Mafia, that is, organized criminals, by using extortion, racketeering, and coercion.

I'll give you an example of members of the LGBTQIA community behaving like a vicious street mob: In August of 2023, the governor of Texas had a ceremonial bill signing with swimming champion Riley Gaines, and a mob of LGBTQIA activists showed up and began viciously attacking Greg Abbott, Riley Gaines, and the other attendees, both physically and verbally, as they were walking into the courthouse. They were throwing water on them, spitting on them, yelling, screaming, and cursing at them, and calling them homophobic names, including the minor children who were with them. This behavior arises from a street mob mentality, and in this case it was intended to intimidate and bully the attendees and stop them from opposing the LGBTQIA community. This proves my point that if you disagree with the LGBTQIA community, question them, oppose them, or have an opinion that is different from theirs, they will send the alphabet mob after you to try to silence you. That's why I call them the "alphabet mob," because they act like a street mob of people who gang up on others in order to force their will on them and ram their ideology down their throats.

Now what was the punishment for these members of the LGBTQIA community who attacked and criminally assaulted Riley Gaines and others? You guessed it, absolutely nothing. The members of the LGBTQIA community felt that they were entitled to criminally assault people as long as they were heterosexual because LGBTQIA people are a so-called "protected class." What happened at the ceremonial bill signing was a heterophobic hate crime. If the situation had been reversed and a group of heterosexuals had assaulted, spit on, and attacked some members of the LGBTQIA community in the same way, then the heterosexuals would have been arrested for a hate crime. Which proves my point that many (not all) in the LGBTQIA community are heterophobic.

You may be saying to yourself right now, *What happened in Texas is not representative of the entire LGBTQIA community.* And you would be right, except that no other members or leaders from the LGBTQIA community group condemned this behavior by their fellow members, meaning that they condoned it by their silence. Why would they refuse to condemn it? Because they want to be able to have this type of tactic available to use anytime they don't get their way, either through the courts or by some other means. They want to intimidate heterosexuals and make them bend to their will so that they can complete the erasing process of heterosexuality and replace it with homosexuality. Don't believe it? Just look around at society today. It's an LGBTQIA takeover.

Again, I call the LGBTQIA community the "alphabet mob" because they use coercion, extortion, and racketeering tactics on any person or any business that opposes them, just like the Mafia does.

Following are definitions and a discussion of Mafia/mob tactics:

Coercion

Coercion is the practice of persuading someone to do something by the use of force or threat.

I'll give you an example of coercion by the LGBTQIA community. What most (not all) in the LGBTQIA community are saying to heterosexuals is, *If you don't celebrate us, side with us, march with us, agree with us, and let us fulfill our agenda and force our will on you, then we will bully you, shame you, smear you, attack you, and destroy your life.* Just like they did with Riley Gaines and the others. Another example of an alphabet mob attack is from May 23, 2023, when a New York City college professor attacked a *New York Post* reporter named Reuben Fenton with a machete for asking her some questions at her home about why she attacked some pro-life protestors at the college. This LGBTQIA member chased the reporter down the street with the machete. Now reverse the two roles, meaning heterosexual and homosexual, and what do you have? A hate crime. So, why isn't this a hate crime? I say that it is a hate crime. It's called heterophobia.

After these two different attacks by a member of the LGBTQIA community against heterosexuals, there was not one word of condemnation from the leaders of the LGBTQIA community. This incident with the member of the LGBTQIA community and a machete is a heterophobic hate crime. If the roles had been reversed and a heterosexual person attacked a member of the LGBTQIA community with a machete, then it would have been considered a hate crime against someone from the LGBTQIA community. Why is what happened not deemed or prosecuted as a heterophobic hate crime? It is because the LGBTQIA community is a so-called "protected class" and the heterosexual community is not. This is an unfair double standard where an LGBTQIA person gets to attack heterosexuals and there are absolutely no consequences for his or her actions. Heterosexuals, it's time to take a stand. You are being bullied into the closet. Take this account into consideration, which is a clear case of heterophobia and also matches the definition of Mafia coercion.

Extortion

Extortion is the practice of obtaining something, especially money, through the use of force or threat.

Let me give you an example of extortion. Most but not all people in the LGBTQIA community extort large corporations. They go to these organizations or businesses and tell them that if they won't make their athletes wear the LGBTQIA community's colors or display the LGBTQIA community's flag on their uniforms, thereby promoting and funding the LGBTQIA community organization, then they will smear their company as homophobic. They tell these companies that if they don't sponsor, meaning fund or give money to, the pride parade, which is the parade celebrating the LGBTQIA community, then they will smear them, boycott their business, and label them as homophobic. The LGBTQIA community demands that politicians back LGBTQIA causes over heterosexual functions, and if they don't comply, then they send the alphabet mob out to attack them and instigate a negative smear campaign against them. That matches the definition of Mafia extortion.

Racketeering

Dealing in obscene matter is one of the thirty-five crimes that qualify as a RICO crime. RICO is short for racketeer influenced and corrupt organizations.

Let me give you an example of LGBTQIA racketeering tactics. Given that one of the possible thirty-one counts of racketeering is dealing in obscene matter, I think going to grade schools and letting drag queens teach our young, impressionable heterosexual children about sex from the homosexual point of view and by using sexually obscene books is indeed dealing in obscene matter. And having a stranger teaching your young children about sex, and in this case, alternative sex, without their parents' knowledge, input, or permission is a gateway for pedophiles to groom heterosexual children for abuse or sexual assault, which should not be done. It is a very bad idea. Who is going to be there to check into the teachers to make sure they are not pedophiles? The answer is no one. That's the definition of "dealing in obscene matter," which is one of the counts of racketeering.

The word *obscene*, an adjective, is "(of the portrayal or description of sexual matters) offensive or disgusting by accepted standards of morality and decency."

Now think about the foregoing two tactics and ask me again why I call the LGBTQIA community the "alphabet mob"? If the shoe fits, wear it.

Members of the LGBTQIA community act as if no one has the right to question them, challenge them, debate them, oppose them, or disagree with them in any way. If any of these things occurs, then they lay down the "victim of homophobia" card to silence and censor people who don't or won't bow down to them. So, they have everyone walking on eggshells and being afraid of them just like the mob! They have a mob-like mentality because, being a protected class, they are inured against harm and harassment, which is fine—there's nothing wrong with that. However, they have carried their being a protected class over to include jokes and anything they dislike that is not even offensive toward them. The problem with that line of thinking is that everyone else, including members of the LGBTQIA community, are laughing at other groups, but at the same time, LGBTQIA people can't laugh at themselves or accept jokes about them that others tell. Just like the LGBTQIA person who attacked Dave Chappelle, the comedian, onstage at one of his shows. Now this LGBTQIA community member was at the show to laugh at jokes about other people and groups, but he manufactured outrage when it came to the jokes Chappelle told about the LGBTQIA community. This individual was there intentionally looking for something to be outraged about so that he could deem himself as a victim and use his supposed victimhood status to manufacture outrage and therefore justify his physical attack on Dave Chappelle and the heterosexual community. This is a case of sheer hypocrisy. We all have the right to freedom of speech, but LGBTQIA community believes that they are above everyone else and in a class by themselves, meaning untouchable like the mob—and therein lies the problem. They believe that they are above criticism and beyond reproach even though they have faults and flaws and even though there are bad, hateful apples in their group just like in every other group. They believe that they shouldn't have to withstand being offended by anything or anyone. However, they think that they get to set the bar determining the level of so-called "offensiveness" they will tolerate, while everyone just has deal with it. The LGBTQIA community believes that they have a right to act out with bad behavior, while the rest of us have to suffer the consequences for our bad behavior.

Members of the LGBTQIA community believe that they can do whatever they want even if it's negative and that they should get a free pass and not be punished for their negative actions. Otherwise, they will cry homophobia, which provides them protection for their negative actions or behavior. In turn, they are deemed as untouchable like a mobster in the alphabet mob.

Again you see why I call them the "alphabet mob." The LGBTQIA community comes at you with a vicious vengeance and tries to destroy your life if they feel that you have offended them, whether it's true or not. But remember, they think that they get to set the bar—and the bar is set so low that it's on the ground. This is done intentionally because members of the LGBTQIA community can't handle any opposition. Whenever they encounter it, they play the victim.

This mentality has echoes of the sympathetic bully. A sympathetic bully lowers the level of what he or she will tolerate down to zero, resulting in his or her inability to handle any opposition. That way, everyone and everything offends this individual. Now he or she can bully the strong people who disagree with him or her, and whom he or she can't measure up to, into submission by claiming that he or she is the victim. Now this person can rally the alphabet mob and get them to attack the people with whom he or she has a problem, by manufacturing victimhood conditions, gaining sympathy, and persuading others to join him or her into bullying the supposed offender, making that person bow down and submit to the LGBTQIA mob by way of the mob's silencing, censoring and canceling the person, getting him or her fired from his or her job, getting him or her taken off social media platforms, and so on.

Look at how powerful this person becomes by manufacturing outrage and turning himself or herself into a supposed victim, becoming the sympathetic bully and making others be his or her emotional keeper, looking out for him or her and making sure that he or she is not offended and/or getting his or her feelings hurt. This happens while the person does absolutely nothing to help himself or herself, such as seeking out therapy or medication to help with any psychological problems or weaknesses, which the individual, and not others, is totally responsible for. The emotional keeper is a con person, making up reasons to bully the people who oppose him or her. Then the alphabet mob turn themselves into supposed victims after getting sympathetic treatment from others, then they become an angry mob, turning on any heterosexuals who oppose them, shutting them up and possibly cutting them off of their livelihoods, destroying their lives. Why? Because the LGBTQIA community is the so-called "protected class," a.k.a. the alphabet mob, who have deemed themselves above heterosexuals and who can destroy your life by any means necessary, manufacturing outrage and becoming the sympathetic bully. Get it now?

We as a society have to put a check on this mob-like mentality and hold the alphabet mob accountable for their negative bullying actions, just like every other person or group in society.

Members of the LGBTQIA community are not above the rest of us and must be treated as such. It is imperative, therefore, that we achieve fairness in our society and ensure that checks and balances are in place. If you disagree with this, I say unto you, "Frankly, I don't give a damn!" We are all equal, so deal with it! And if you, the alphabet mob, still believe that you are above the rest of us, then society will have no choice but to cancel you. Don't believe it? Ask Dylan Mulvaney and Bud Light! Bud Light sales have tanked because Budweiser didn't understand, or else took for granted, its core heterosexual market and tried to replace it with an LGBTQIA market. This effort failed miserably. Heterosexuals proved to Bud Light that they will not be erased from the market. Ask yourself this question: If the LGBTQIA community was more important as a customer than heterosexuals, then why didn't the LGBTQIA community meet the current sales rate and thereby stop Bud Light stock from falling? Bud Light acquiesced to the alphabet mob's extortion tactics and lost. The LGBTQIA community tried to bully their way into corporate America and erase heterosexuality, and it cost Bud Light the number one spot in beer sales and billions of dollars in lost market share. Target tried to appeal to the LGBTQIA community too, with the tuck-friendly swimsuit, an LGBTQIA version, or so-called "trans man" female swimsuit. That didn't work either. The failure of the tuck-friendly swimsuit was the result of heterosexuals taking a stand and saying that enough is enough: no more forcing the LGBTQIA takeover agenda down our throats. I know that most, not all, members of the LGBTQIA community will call all this offensive and homophobic. However, that is an accusation taken from the bullying playbook that they always run to when they can't get their way, measure up to others, or debate an issue on its merits. But this tactic is not going to work with me, because I know this con game up, down, and back and forth. That's why I wrote *The LGBTQIA Community and Betrayal*, in order to expose the behavior of the LGBTQIA community to the heterosexual community so that the latter can take a stand!

Chapter 6

LGBTQIA vs. God: The Leftists' Religion and Their War against the Church

Tyranny of the minority—a culture of oppression and harsh and unjust acts.

The LGBTQIA community does not get to ram their identity or ideology down our throats and bully heterosexuals into the closet. We get to decide our own identity and beliefs.

In today's society, God, the church, and other religious institutions are being attacked to appease and please the LGBTQIA community. People of the Far Left in this country are attacking religion and its institutions for one reason and one reason alone: because LGBTQIA is their religion, believe it or not. What do I mean? Every time a religious institution has something to say to society about morality and our need to act accordingly, the LGBTQIA community comes out against it. Why do they always oppose God, Christ, and other religious figures? I'll tell you why: because the immoral things they do go against God and religious morals, and in order to keep doing what they do, that is, behaving immorally, they need to discredit God and religion. They have to protect their side in any given situation and by any means necessary, including intimidation, bullying, smearing the church, and smearing heterosexuals' religious beliefs. But what are they protecting? And why are most (not all) of them against God? In our society, we have Catholics, Protestants, Jews, Muslims, and people of other religions, and the leftists have put up the LGBTQIA community to counter and oppose these religions. Why? Because LGBTQIA is the leftists' religion, so they put LGBTQIA in the category with the other religions. Believe it or not! If you don't believe it, then tell me why the leftists always put the LGBTQIA community up to oppose every religion? Tell me why, if anyone brings up morals, the leftists counter the argument with LGBTQIA concerns? If anyone brings up the church, they counter it with LGBTQIA concerns. Their thing is that they have to protect the LGBTQIA community. But from what? I'll tell you from what: sin. Because those among the LGBTQIA community know deep down that what they're doing is sinful, meaning neither right nor immoral. They know that on some level that something is wrong with their lifestyle. However, they have to put up a front and fight off religion in order to justify their continuing to do what they are currently doing—that is, normalize it.

And not only do they have to fight any and all religions, but also they have to fight off God himself. God destroyed Sodom and Gomorrah for the same exact thing that the LGBTQIA community stands for and what they are about. So, the leftists have made LGBTQIA their religion and their religious fight, because most (not all) members of the LGBTQIA community do not accept God or religion. By making LGBTQIA their religion, now they can be accepted. God made man and woman so that we can be fruitful, procreating and multiplying. They LGBTQIA community will end the human race because they are unable to procreate. Two men can't procreate, and two women can't either. With the LGBTQIA paradigm successful, society will destroy itself and die out. This means that the LGBTQIA community has to have heterosexuals to procreate in order to stay alive and keep their community alive. Yet at the same time they are trying to erase heterosexuality, its values, and everything it stands for.

It makes no sense, unless you consider who is currently running the country. Somehow the people in power have convinced themselves that heterosexuals should be more like LGBTQIA people rather than the other way around. It's all about power and control—and this is the betrayal. The LGBTQIA community preaches inclusion, but not if you disagree with them, at which point you become excluded and are subjected to being bullied, smeared, shamed, and destroyed. I find it interesting that many (not all) in the LGBTQIA community are willing to discriminate against heterosexuals but at the same time don't want heterosexuals to discriminate against them. It's sheer hypocrisy. They have deemed themselves as the ultimate authority figure over everyone because of their protected class status. Things have swung too far in the LGBTQIA community's favor to the point where they have taken away the First Amendment right to free speech from heterosexuals. I saw on *Fox News* on July 19, 2023, that an Arizona State University donor had asked for his donation to the university back because some LGBTQIA students would not allow him to speak, not liking his faith-based message. The ASU dean came out the next day and made an announcement on DEI (diversity, equity, and inclusion), which was totally hypocritical and dismissive of what had happened to the donor who wanted to donate more than one hundred thousand dollars. The dean, fearing repercussions from the LGBTQIA community, sided with them. The alphabet mob had succeeded at intimidating the donor and the dean.

I wonder, if someone were to bully the alphabet mob like they bully others who disagree with them, what would they say or do? I'm sure that they would claim homophobia and discrimination. But somehow they are protected when they do the same thing—the same intimidation, bullying, and discriminatory behavior, in this case called heterophobia. They preach to other religious groups as if they are in church. That's because LGBTQIA is their church and is also their religion. It's like a cult.

As a cult, the members of the LGBTQIA community still fall into line even when what they are doing is wrong and even if it hurts the LGBTQIA community or goes against its best interests, for example, what happened with Bud Light and Dylan Mulvaney. Anytime a person falls into line when the situation is bad for them and then this destroys their livelihood, it's a cult.

Some readers likely will say that my calling the LGBTQIA community a cult is homophobic. If they say that, then they will be making my point by playing the sympathetic bully. Calling people homophobic for pointing out facts or the truth is a dog whistle for the alphabet mob to attack the messenger or the person whom they disagree with. Religious groups come in many types and forms. Just because LGBTQIA is a gender-based religion doesn't mean it's not a religion. It just happens to be the leftists' and the LGBTQIA community's religion. Believe it or not.

Chapter 7

The Bible and God's Morals Sodom and Gomorrha The Anti-Christ

Tyranny of the minority—a culture of oppression and harsh and unjust acts.

The LGBTQIA community does not get to ram their identity or ideology down our throats and bully heterosexuals into the closet. We get to decide our own identity and beliefs.

The devil's greatest trick was to make people believe that he did not exist.

God destroyed Sodom and Gomorrah because human beings had perverted themselves through promiscuous behavior and homosexuality.

God made Adam and Eve and not Adam and Steve.

The foregoing are just a few quotes illustrating society today or beliefs from the Bible. These are the beliefs that keep our society moral and from going down the road of the Antichrist, according to the Bible. Now the heterosexual community's moral beliefs are what many in our society live by and what this great nation was built upon: Christian values. These values stop people from becoming immoral.

They stop some from living in wedlock, stops some from having an unwanted pregnancy from living in wedlock, and stops some from having abortions, that is, killing innocent babies inside the womb. Now those who believe in abortion make the argument that it is a woman's choice to carry a pregnancy to term or not because it is her body. But such people still have to get past the moral issue in order to commit this gruesome act. To do this, they have to reject God and dismiss their religious beliefs.

Moral beliefs also stop people from becoming homosexual. And therein lies the problem for the LGBTQIA community: if they follow the moral beliefs of the Bible, then they mustn't have gay sex or homosexual relationships. Therefore, they have to attack the Bible, tear it down, and totally destroy it. This is how most (not all) members of the LGBTQIA community deal with or get past the moral test of religion. They minimize the heterosexual community's faith God. They want to get heterosexuals to cease abiding by their own faith in God. They want to bully heterosexuals into dismissing or destroying their Bible-based religious beliefs. They figure that if they get the heterosexuals to go against their own religious beliefs, then they can fill the resulting vacuum with the beliefs of the LGBTQIA community, at which time they will be able to go on and destroy God and religion as a whole, and then recruit indoctrinate the heterosexual community with gay beliefs and erase the heterosexuals' religion altogether. The key is to get heterosexuals to attack and subsequently dismiss their own religion or religious beliefs.

Members of the LGBTQIA community never approach the real issue head-on and try to fix the real problem of being gay. There are a lot of gay people who don't want to be gay, whom the LGBTQIA community will try to shame and force out of the closet because they want them to be a part of the group as there is strength in numbers.

But some of these individuals want to maintain their own identity and don't want to be a part of the LGBTQIA community or advance the LGBTQIA community's agenda, from schools to statehouses to federal government buildings and anywhere else they see fit.

By outing prominent homosexuals who wish to keep their private lives private, the LGBTQIA community can be accepted in all areas of our society, and then they can complete their erasing of heterosexuality from society and replacing it with the LGBTQIA community and its new world order. Heterosexuals, take a stand!

I ask, who do you know who would want such a thing to take place? According to the Bible, the answer is the Antichrist—Satan, the devil, or whatever you want to call him. Now I'm not calling the LGBTQIA community the Antichrist, but I am saying that it sounds a lot like the Antichrist as described in the Bible. I believe that the stigma that the LGBTQIA community is the Antichrist, or evil, or unholy, is what the LGBTQIA community is trying to erase from our society, but the heterosexual community is in their way. So, they have set out to destroy the heterosexual community altogether without making it appear as if they are attacking religion or people of faith.

It's an extreme, backdoor way of eliminating God, religion, and the church in one fell swoop. Doing that will erase heterosexuality and replace it with homosexuality, and then the LGBTQIA community will have completed the master plan of betrayal. Heterosexuals, take a stand! What I posit here may explain why the vulgar behavior of the Sisters of Perpetual Indulgence and their immoral blasphemy against, and mocking of, the Catholic Church was met with not a word of condemnation from the LGBTQIA community. Because the Sisters of Perpetual Indulgence are doing the LGBTQIA community's dirty work. That work involves tearing down God, religion, and people of faith without its appearing as if the LGBTQIA community has put its stamp of approval on it.

When the bad actors from the LGBTQIA community do negative things, you never hear of the LGBTQIA community leadership condemning them. Why not? The excuse they always use is that speaking out would create homophobia and violence against the LGBTQIA community. l call this an excuse because, having listened closely to their so-called reasoning, I have noticed that what they are doing is shifting responsibility for their own negative behavior onto heterosexuals, actually blaming heterosexuals for their own members' negative actions. The LGBTQIA community is saying that if they condemn or punish their own bad actors, then the heterosexual community will discriminate and commit acts of violence against them. Wow, that's an amazing deflection. According to the LGBTQIA community, none of their members may be punished by anyone for their negative behavior or any crimes they commit against heterosexuals, otherwise it will be considered homophobia.

On May 28, 2023, a transgender person named Audrey Hale shot up a Christian school in Nashville, Tennessee, killing six, including schoolchildren. This transgender person, Hale left a note stating why she did this. However, leftist politicians and the police refused to let the public see the note, saying that it would inflame the heterosexual community and cause them to oppose the LGBTQIA community— and they didn't want the LGBTQIA community to be seen in a negative light. This incident helps make my point. Here, the authorities chose to protect the LGBTQIA community, deflect attention away from the real issue, and blame the heterosexual community for the negative action of one member of the LGBTQIA community, even though this individual killed six heterosexual people in what I believe to be a heterosexual hate crime. Now if the situation were reversed, would the LGBTQIA community, the leftist politicians, and the police have protected the heterosexual community by declining to share the killer's note confessing to a hate crime? You and I both know that the answer is no! Voilà, a member of the LGBTQIA community gets off scot-free after committing a heterosexual hate crime! This means that as long as the crime is against a heterosexual, it isn't considered a hate crime. This is a betrayal.

The fact that the laws are currently configured in this way also explains why the LGBTQIA community feels that they can get away with treating heterosexuals badly or bullying them. It may also explain why the LGBTQIA community feels that they can erase heterosexuality at will with no backlash against their members. It may explain why the LGBTQIA community is placing their own version of women, that is, transgender males, in positions over heterosexual women. It may also explain why the LGBTQIA community wants heterosexuals to acknowledge their own version of a mother, a.k.a. a pregnant man or "birthing person," over the heterosexuals' version. This may explain why they want to have drag queen story hour in grade school, preaching homosexuality. This may explain why they believe that it's OK to allow biological males who are now transgender women to play biological women's sports. And this explains the betrayal of the heterosexual community and the LGBTQIA community's wanting to erase heterosexuals and replace them with their own homosexual versions. It explains everything about the LGBTQIA mentality and their agenda of bullying heterosexuals into the closet, because they feel themselves to be above being punished for their negative behavior or actions. And they blame and shame the heterosexual community and deflect responsibility onto them as if it's their fault. Heterosexuals, take a stand, because the Antichrist has revealed itself through the Sisters of Perpetual Indulgence. Most, but not all, members of the LGBTQIA community are trying to erase and/or destroy heterosexuality by way of your religious faith. Heterosexuals, you have been betrayed.

Chapter 8

LGBTQIA and Avoiding Heterosexual Pronouns—Gender Identity, Neopronouns, and Nonbinary Ideology: Erasing Heterosexuality into Extinction

Tyranny of the minority—a culture of oppression and harsh and unjust acts.

The LGBTQIA community does not get to ram their identity or ideology down our throats and bully heterosexuals into the closet. We get to decide our own identity and beliefs.

Many, but not all, members of the LGBTQIA community want to erase heterosexuality and force it into extinction. What do I mean? Some members of the LGBTQIA community want other people to call them *they* and *them* rather than *he* and *him* or *she* and *her*. These people don't want any part of a heterosexual identity. They also want to erase all heterosexual names and concepts from society. Now there are people who identify as things and subsequently refer to themselves by neopronouns, things such as leaves, bells, rocks, mountains, birds, volcanoes, hurricanes, rainbows, or turtles. Get the point? In other words, they'll take any identity but a heterosexual identity, the aim being to erase heterosexuals from existence. And some of these people want to make it a crime for any heterosexual who disagrees with them, misidentifies them, or chooses not to call them by their preferred pronoun.

Such individuals want these heterosexuals who behave this way toward them so they can have them fired from their jobs, taken off social media, locked up in jail, or canceled in some other fashion. This is not the American way, as we all have the right to free speech, meaning we are at liberty to express our own opinions and, even more important, to be wrong. Some members of the LGBTQIA community don't want heterosexuals to think for themselves or to have their own religion or their own opinions. They want to be the ones who decide who gets to speak and what they say and how they may it, thereby erasing the heterosexuals' right to free speech, the first and most potent thing that they want to erase. The second objective is to sway heterosexuals toward groupthink. There are some powerful people in the LGBTQIA community who are saying that they are authority figures, meaning that they are bosses or the arbiters of free speech, and they get to tell heterosexuals what they can say, when they can say it, and how they can say it. And if they fail to comply, the LGBTQIA community will smear them, shame them, bully them, and force them into compliance and into the closet. Again, this is erasing your right to free speech.

Now some powerful people in the LGBTQIA community also want to erase heterosexual gender identity. Let's start with the heterosexual woman. What is the definition of a woman? The LGBTQIA community can't or doesn't want to describe what a woman is. Why? Because their aim is to erase heterosexual women and replace them with transgender women. Don't believe it? Then ask yourself why they don't want to define or describe what a heterosexual woman is. Why do they call pregnant women "birthing people," rather than "women" or "mothers"? Why are they replacing biological women with transgender women and pushing for the latter's inclusion in advertisements over traditional heterosexual women, for example, Dylan Mulvaney being named the spokesperson for Bud Light. There is a transgender-influencer makeup artist for Maybelline cosmetics, and Target is marketing the tuck-friendly swimsuit for transgender women. Ask yourself why the leftists in our society don't defend heterosexual women in sports, whom they claim to be champions of? Instead they push for and promote the inclusion of transgender women, that is, biological men, over traditional heterosexual women. Just to name a few of these people: we have a leftist Supreme Court justice Ketanji Brown Jackson pretending that she can't define what a woman is, even though she is a woman herself. Ask any leftist, and that includes many (not all) on the LGBTQIA side of the aisle, to define a woman, and they will play dumb and pretend that they don't know what one is. Why? Because this the another step toward erasing heterosexuality from existence. How is this occurring? There is no pushback and no opposing voices, because everyone is too afraid of the leftist alphabet mob's attacking them, trying to intimidate them, smear them, and bully them into compliance, into submission, and into the closet. If these tactics fail, the LGBTQIA community will use the "sympathetic bully" approach to get the alphabet mob to attack, again to complete their transition of society, erasing heterosexuality, replacing it with homosexuality, and taking over our society. It's a betrayal, a hostile takeover, and a case of tyranny of the minority. In other words, only the LGBTQIA community gets to make and set all the rules in society. Things are how they want it. Do as they say or you will be canceled or destroyed. Heterosexuals are the ones targeted for erasure. It's like that movie with Arnold Schwarzenegger and Vanessa Williams called *Eraser* where an elite group of people in government seek to erase those who pose a threat to their agenda of power and control and therefore must be eliminated. It's a move from the same playbook used by the LGBTQIA community, except the aim of the latter is not literally to kill people, but to kill gender. In this case, the objective is to erase heterosexuality, meaning kill heterosexuality, and replace it with homosexuality, a process that the LGBTQIA community has chosen to start with women. However, the men will not be excepted. They will be erased too.

There are some feminists and some in positions of leadership in the LGBTQIA community who are one and the same, who are calling strong, confident masculine men "toxic," saying that they exhibit "toxic masculinity." Why? Because it's the best way they have found to get men to doubt their own confidence and strength, which is necessary because the average feminist or transgender woman can't measure up to the naturally high confidence level and strength of men. Look at Lia Thomas, the transgender swimmer. This guy, and I say guy because he still has his penis, was a middle-of-the-road men's swimmer unable to measure up to the highly masculine men who were actually his peers who entered the sport of women's swimming and did his part, which was to obliterate all the records and accomplishments of the heterosexual women who had competed before him. Notice I said his part. I'm talking about the part that some (not all) members of the LGBTQIA community want Lia Thomas and others like him to play—a part in the LGBTQIA community's master plan to erase the heterosexual community.

Some of the powers that be among the LGBTQIA community have waged an all-out war, a tyranny-of-the-minority-style assault on the heterosexual community, and they are willing to do whatever it takes to win this war, including ensuring the takedown of heterosexual women by refusing even to acknowledge them as women, or as mothers. Instead, these people are saying that a man can get pregnant. Which defies logic. So, they are gaslighting the public and purposely confusing the country with this false ideology. And they are seeking punishment for you, if you as a heterosexual person refuse to comply. It's a tyrannical assault waged by the minority to erase heterosexuals, both men and women. How can a man get pregnant? He can't. He doesn't have the body parts to develop a baby; only women do. What the LGBTQIA community are calling pregnant men are actually women who pretended to be men and then got pregnant by a man. I say this because no woman has any sperm with which to fertilize the egg of another woman. So, to say that men can get pregnant is to engage in gaslighting, a game of pretend game that the LGBTQIA community is playing with heterosexuals. The goal is to confuse everyone, just like they are confused, in order to pull off their deceitful plan to erase heterosexuality.

Even White House press secretary Karine Jean-Pierre got into the deceitful heterosexual-erasing game. She was asked why President Joe Biden has chosen not to defend biological women's rights in sports. Her response was, "It's complicated. There is no right or wrong answer." Why would she give such a confusing answer? I'll tell you why. It's because she is a lesbian. She is a member of the LGBTQIA community who is help to push the cause of erasing heterosexuality. She just happens to be the White House press secretary. However, she is gay! Still, the LGBTQIA community wants heterosexuals to help them do the job for them by acquiescing to their gaslighting and allowing them to play their con game. Heterosexuals, don't fall for the con game, because it's a scam. The LGBTQIA community wants you to kill off your own heterosexuality. Take a stand! The so-called "nonbinary" people don't want you to lock them into any one gender category. Why? Because then they wouldn't be able to choose which gender they say they are whenever it behooves them to identify as one gender or the other. If they don't like something and they find that their gender is hindering them in some form or fashion from eradicating that thing, then they can just switch their gender and get a more favorable outcome—another gaslighting con game played by some, but not all, members of the LGBTQIA community. What they want is to set the rules so that they can win every time, but also, and more important so that heterosexuals will lose every time. These LGBTQIA community members or so-called "nonbinary" or "neopronoun" people don't want to have any accountability requirements placed on them. They want the heterosexuals to be their "emotional keepers." In other words, they want to make everyone but themselves responsible for how they feel, while at the same time they do absolutely nothing to help themselves or strengthen themselves emotionally and mentally via therapy or medication. They want heterosexuals to act like caretakers of their emotions, gauging how they feel at any given moment and giving them the positive outcome they seek. Any heterosexuals who fail to serve them in this way will be held accountable for their feelings and the outcome, or so say the emotional keepers. This is why the LGBTQIA community calls everyone and everything offensive, so they can manufacture outrage and get someone who is opposing them to bow down to them and change his or her language to fit that of the emotional keeper so that the latter can feel better about themselves. But more importantly, they seek to cause the heterosexual to feel guilty or bad about himself or herself and adjust his or her language and lifestyle to conform to that of the so-called "victim." It's a con game played by this type of person.

The scenario is as follows: everyone else has to do all the work and change for the "victim," while he or she sits back and dictates to heterosexuals how they should behave and speak, in such a way that pleases the "victim," doing absolutely nothing about his or her own weaknesses, emotional damage, selfishness, and low self-esteem. These people who play the victim are the slackers and the misfits of the world. They epitomize an emotional keeper. There are therapists, psychiatrists, and medication available to help people like this.

While everyone else has to raise their tolerance level toward people who hold opinions opposite to theirs, the members of the LGBTQIA community have intentionally lowered their tolerance level down to zero and are now unable to handle any individual or any opposition. Therefore, now they can claim to be a supposed victim of the smallest and most insignificant actions of the heterosexual community. Why would they want to do that? It's because they want to become sympathetic bullies. Remember, the sympathetic bully has great power by becoming a supposed victim. Now he or she can get sympathy from others and subsequently get those sympathizers to gang up on and bully the person who is opposing him or her, sending them out to attack this person like a pit bull for hurting the feelings of the poor so-called "victim." It's a con game played by certain kinds of people, and it's how the LGBTQIA community gets other people and other communities to do their dirty work for them, so they themselves get to avoid actually looking like the real bully. The plan is to get the sympathizers to bully the person who is in opposition to the so-called "victim," with the sympathizers shaming this person, getting him or her canceled from social media platforms, getting him or her fired from jobs, and doing whatever else they see fit to take away from the opposition. It's a clever strategy, but it shows how emotionally and mentally weak the people who use it are. And it's not going to work with me, because I know the con of the sympathetic bully. And I'm exposing it here in *The LGBTQIA Community and Betrayal* so that others can fight against and push back toward these con artists, the ones who try to get people to self-censor and who push people into the closet and erase their heterosexuality from existence, just so they can have their own way anytime they want.

This chapter explored just one of the things that some members of the LGBTQIA community are using to erase heterosexuality, namely, the sympathetic bully and the emotional keeper tactic. If you don't know what I mean, then reread chapter 3.

Chapter 9

LGBTQIA—Deceptively Labeling Heterosexual Children as "Trans Kids," Recruiting and Indoctrinating Heterosexual Children in order to Transform Them into Being Gay, and Opening the Door to Gay Pedophiles

Tyranny of the minority—a culture of oppression and harsh and unjust acts.

The LGBTQIA community does not get to ram their identity or ideology down our throats and bully heterosexuals into the closet. We get to decide our own identity and beliefs.

What is a trans kid? How does a kid know that he or she is gay? How does he or she know that a certain girl is not just a tomboy or that a certain boy doesn't merely have feminine ways and that they both may never grow out of these things? Nobody knows the answer to these questions, which fact is why children shouldn't be allowed to make permanent life-changing decisions without the knowledge and aid of their parents. The LGBTQIA community has waged a campaign that recruits kids at the grade school level, indoctrinates them, and transforms them from heterosexual children into homosexual children, all while keeping it a secret from their parents, meaning it's done without the parents' knowledge or consent.

Some among the LGBTQIA community want children under the age of ten to be granted the right to make their own decisions on permanent gender-altering surgery. A ten-year-old making his own decision on whether or not to have his penis surgically removed without his parents' knowledge or consent? Are you kidding me! Remember that a teacher is not even authorized to give an aspirin to a child without the consent of his or her parents, but the school and teachers are able to help a ten-year-old make a decision about major permanent body-altering surgery? This makes no sense. Also, the schools can help minor students get puberty blockers, a medication that stops a male child from going into puberty, which otherwise would turn him from a boy into a man. Basically, it's chemical castration. So, the LGBTQIA community wants to stop male children from becoming fully developed men or else turn them into girls, again without their parents' knowledge or permission.

Now why would the LGBTQIA community want these things for a child, whose mind or brain is not fully developed yet? There's only one reason for this: because they want to erase and destroy the heterosexual community, literally by going after those in their infancy. A reader might argue, saying that this is not true and that the LGBTQIA community only wants to help trans kids to realize their identity. The problem with this belief it is impossible for a ten-year-old to know that he or she is gay. Some girls are tomboys and some boys have feminine ways at that age, and they grow out of it later in life. Now how is that ten-year-old going to cope with the psychological damage and problems later on in life when he or she decide that he or she really wasn't gay, that it was just a faze he or she was going through? Well, then it'll be too late and the damage will have been done. Now who is going to help this person overcome the physical and psychological trauma of having had his penis or her breasts removed? The school officials and teachers who recruited, indoctrinated, and brainwashed this individual? No! The doctor who did the surgery and profited from child body mutilation? No! The LGBTQIA community who sacrificed the child like a sheep to wolves like some satanic cult? No! It's going to be the parents, the very ones who were not informed, who will be left to pick up the pieces, holding the bag of their permanently damaged child with a twisted sense of gender identity thanks to ideological indoctrination by the LGBTQIA community. It's going to be the parents, who were bullied and told to shut up and let their kids make their own decisions, who were systemically replaced by the school board members, teachers, and doctors, who had no knowledge of what was happening, and who were intentionally kept in the dark as their ten-year-old boy was being turned into a girl, who will be left to try to undo the mountains of damage.

How do ten-year-olds know about puberty blockers? The answer is that they don't. Someone has to tell them. And in most cases, someone has to coach them into taking puberty-blocking medications or having permanent body-altering surgery. This is done all in secret and without the parents' knowledge or consent. Now why would anyone want to help a child as young as ten years old do such things without asking the child's parents for permission? I'll tell you why. It's because the parents would put a stop to it and do what's best for their child. The LGBTQIA community is doing what's best for their community, which is to erase and destroy the heterosexual community by starting with its youngest members, that is, minor children, while at the same time adding to or strengthening their own community with the inclusion of these children into their group. So now the LGBTQIA community is bullying parents out of their own children's lives, children for whom the parents are responsible in every way except for the LGBTQIA community's way, in essence telling them to shut up and go into the closet. This is a betrayal by the LGBTQIA community. The alphabet mob is the protector of the LGBTQIA community, sent out by the LGBTQIA community like a vicious guard dog to attack parents, intimidating them, bullying them, and stopping them from protecting their own children. And if anyone tries to push back or fight them, then the alphabet mob will claim homophobia and will then take on the role of the sympathetic bully, pretending to be a so-called "victim" of heterosexuality and trying to get any LGBTQIA sympathizers to attack this person too. Who do you believe knows what is best for a minor child? The parents who bore the child, lived with him or her, and raised him or her, or the LGBTQIA community, who wants to recruit children and indoctrinate them? I say it's the parents. If you believe it's the LGBTQIA community, then I ask you: Who the hell do you think you are? God? You do not get to decide what's best for someone else's children, especially when it comes to permanently damaging them both sexually and mentally, because that psychological or mental damage will be there for a lifetime. You do not get to dictate to parents about their own children. You don't get to take minor children and shape them into your own image. And I say image for a reason: because that's what God does, shapes humankind into his image. This is why I believe that this is the LGBTQIA movement is a leftist religious cult.

A reader may be thinking that what I'm saying is homophobic. It's not. I know the con game and the intimidation game that the alphabet mob tries to play. I know how the victim game is played too. I know about the sympathetic bully, which is a tactic they might use to get everyone against me and try to cancel me, censor me, silence me, and force me into the closet. This way, the voices of those among the LGBTQIA community will be the only ones that are heard. So that tactic is not going to work on me. Calling me names and trying to shame me so that I back down is not going to work with me. Why? Because I'm exposing the truth by stating the facts. I'm just pushing back in order to allow others to have a say in their own children's lives. And if I have to go it alone or even take one for the team, then so be it! I'll do that in order to persevere parents' rights and to stop the extinction of heterosexuality.

I don't hate the LGBTQIA community, and I am not homophobic. I'm happy to let the LGBTQIA community live the way they want to live. I'm not trying to stop them from thriving and achieving their financial or personal goals. However, I'm not going to allow them to stop me or others from discussing issues relevant to us, pursuing our goals, celebrating our achievements, or living the way we want to live. The problem is that these two lifestyles can't coexist according to the LGBTQIA community, so they have to eliminate the enemy, which is the heterosexual community. We can agree to disagree and leave it at that. I'm not going to be intimidated or bullied out of exercising my right to free speech. But I am going to help those who are afraid to push back against the alphabet mob, who are trying to have it only their way. Everyone is equal under the law, and everyone has the right to speak his or her mind. I say "his or her" because there are only two genders regardless of what anyone else may think. You may be saying right now, "That's homophobic." If so, then all you're doing is making my point for me, as clearly you don't want me or anyone else to have their own opinions or point of view. If you believe that there are more than two genders, then you have every right to believe that. However, you can't force me to believe it or ram your belief down my throat. The problem is that you try to.

I know the con game. The purpose of the con game is to confuse everyone, just like the LGBTQIA community is confused, and that way their agenda will be given precedence and ultimately will be carried out. Well, I'm not confused. Sorry, but I don't agree with the LGBTQIA way of thinking. I have my own mind and my own thoughts and beliefs. So do others. And we will decide what's best for us and our children. Not you! The LGBTQIA community may not like that, but too bad: it's our right. So deal with it. And if you have a problem with us and our own beliefs, then once again, you have proven my point, which is that the LGBTQIA community is seeking to have heterosexuality erased, which is a betrayal. Otherwise, why would anyone have a problem with other people's beliefs? The LGBTQIA community is not the arbiter of the right to free speech and others' beliefs. The problem is that they think they are. And I will leave them with it. Because I and others don't owe them anything! That includes trying to turn our children to be like them. We will decide what our children do, not you. And if you don't like that or disagree with it, I don't give a damn. Again, we as a society don't own you anything. Parents are responsible for their own children, and not the LGBTQIA community, which is interfering in heterosexual parents' business and their rights. This will only cause heterosexual parents to start infringing on the LGBTQIA community's lifestyle and rights. So be careful what you ask for, because you just may get it.

We heterosexuals want to be left alone and want to state how we feel, not what the LGBTQIA community wants us to feel. I remember when the LGBTQIA community used to say, "Don't tell us how to live our lives. And stay out of our bedrooms." They seemed to be earnest about it too. What happened to that? Now these same individuals want to come into heterosexual parents' houses and recruit and indoctrinate their children. How hypocritical is that? In others words, it's ow "Do as I say, not as I do" and "Rules for thee but not for me." The LGBTQIA community wants a two-tier justice system, one tier of which allows them to make the rules and pass the laws for others, especially heterosexuals, to follow. They are trying to erase heterosexuality from existence.

Children are very impressionable at grade school age, which fact the LGBTQIA community knows. That's why they are targeting children at that age. I'm old enough to remember back in the late eighties and early nineties when the gay community targeted seven-year-olds in the second grade. There was a big uproar among parents because the LGBTQIA community wanted to teach these very impressionable children about homosexuality by using books. These books about homosexuality and the teachers who wanted to teach them had already been embedded in the schools. Now I have a question: who are those children, and where are they now?

I'll tell you who they are. They are the millennial generation, the most progay sympathizers in LGBTQIA history. Why are they this way? Because they are the children who were targeted, recruited, and indoctrinate by the LGBTQIA community. Now history is trying to repeat itself. Why? Because the LGBTQIA community now has a blueprint for recruiting and indoctrinating children. However, this time the effort is on a massive scale and is intended to permanently erase, eliminate, and destroy the heterosexual community and lifestyle and replace it with the LGBTQIA version of community and lifestyle. The goal is to get to the children and get them to go against their own parents. Use puberty blockers and change their gender at will with no one to oppose them and thereby carry out the LGBTQIA community's agenda, which is to bully the heterosexual community into the closet and to erase them into extinction.

If you don't believe that what I'm saying is true, then tell me where I am wrong. Is this not what is happening in schools today in July 2023? Sure it is. Some people will try to deflect and say that the intention of the LGBTQIA community is not to gaslight you or fool you into believing them, but the facts say otherwise. Now what am I supposed to believe, the facts on the ground in our schools, or my lying ears and eyes? The facts are the facts. I mean, you may not like what I'm saying, and you may not like the fact that I'm exposing the hidden agenda of the LGBTQIA community, but you and no one else can tell me that I'm lying about the facts. The proof is in the schools. I imagine that some people after hearing of *The LGBTQIA Community and Betrayal* will try to intimidate and bully me into submission. But it's not going to work. I know that there are a lot of powerful people in the LGBTQIA community who will try to cancel me or my book and try and stop the public from seeing *The LGBTQIA Community and Betrayal* and reading it, but if they do so, they will only make my point that they are the alphabet mob, who want to erase and destroy the heterosexual community, forcing it into the closet. But that won't stop me speaking the truth as supported by facts and data.

Parents, wake up. Your children are being targeted in order to destroy your beliefs and your heterosexual gender. If you don't take a stand now, then soon your own children will be against you, sent by the LGBTQIA community to destroy you.

The LGBTQIA community is like a cult with brainwashed followers. Yes, I said cult, because the LGBTQIA community wants followers who fall in line and choose not to think for themselves. They want to do the thinking for you. They want minor children to follow them down a path of destruction, even though this will separate and divide these children from their own parents. It will physically, psychologically, and permanently damage them, crippling them as adults. The LGBTQIA community really doesn't give a damn about these children's well-being, only that they join the cultlike group and help them to erase and destroy the heterosexual community and its lifestyle. (LGBTQIA is a cult, and this is their religion.)

There is no such thing as a trans kid. The LGBTQIA community is indoctrinating these kids and making them believe they are transgender. I know this is true because a kid at that age has no clue who he or she is as a person. Someone has to teach the child this, and the LGBTQIA community is trying to beat parents to the punch by keeping secrets from them, which is exclusion and not inclusion. That way the kids will be homosexual and not heterosexual, or else an LGBTQIA sympathizer, which means that the LGBTQIA community will have erased heterosexuals from existence and bullied parents into the closet.

Heterosexuals, your own children will turn on you and start to attack you once they have been indoctrinated into this cultlike religion, a.k.a. the LGBTQIA community, that goes against your heterosexual values and everything that you stand for, so you had better take a stand now and save your children. Or you can be afraid of the alphabet mob and fall in line just like the cult member they want you to be. Remember, a cult demands that its followers fall into line even though it goes against their own best interests, and that's what we have going on here with the LGBTQIA community and heterosexual children. Take a stand now! Why? Because the schools and this mentality make for the perfect playground for LGBTQIA indoctrination and child-molesting pedophiles. When an adult stranger in the school who just happens to be the students' teacher is allowed to discuss explicit graphic sexual matters with your innocent, impressionable child, this is an invitation for pedophiles to gain access to your children. This is a disaster waiting to happen. It is a terrible idea. Whoever agrees with such a decision hasn't thought it through at all. Remember, your child is going to be the lab rat in this experiment. This idea of having an explicit homosexual curriculum in grade school is a pedophile's dream and a magnet drawing the pedophile toward the teaching profession. Again, heterosexuals, take a stand now!

Chapter 10

The LGBTQIA Community and Cancel Culture: The Gateway to Bullying Heterosexuals into the Closet

Tyranny of the minority—a culture of oppression and harsh and unjust acts.

The LGBTQIA community does not get to ram their identity or ideology down our throats and bully heterosexuals into the closet. We get to decide our own identity and beliefs.

The LGBTQIA community is one of the leaders of cancel culture. Anytime a LGBTQIA person doesn't like something that a person from the heterosexual community does, his or her first instinct is to get the individual fired from any job and canceled from all platforms. This is the bullying tactic of the alphabet mob, the tyranny of the minority that the LGBTQIA community uses to erase heterosexuality, control heterosexuals, and push them into the closet.

The LGBTQIA community will deem anything that they dislike as offensive or homophobic and then go and tell any authority figure related to the situation to silence heterosexuals' voices, whether the story is true or false (or just made up and manufactured!). Many among the LGBTQIA community know that there is great power in canceling out heterosexuals' voices. Remember, many members of the LGBTQIA members community (not all) have betrayed heterosexuals and waged a war on heterosexuality. Heterosexuals have been asleep at the wheel, and now this betrayal and this war on heterosexuality has reached almost every area of our society. Heterosexuals are far behind and are fighting a losing battle, as many of the LGBTQIA community's leaders are fighting in a deceitful way. They are tying heterosexuals' hands behind their backs and handicapping them, and putting this biased, underhanded, and unfair treatment under the umbrella of DEI (diversity, equity, and inclusion) along with empowerment and equality! All in the response to so-called "offensiveness" and homophobia. The reason the LGBTQIA community is doing this is to make it appear as if heterosexuals are attacking homosexuals and committing a hate crime against the LGBTQIA community. That way heterosexuals can't combat this unfair treatment by the LGBTQIA community, who now are thusly enabled to bully straight people into the closet.

However, the reality is different. This is a psychological con game played by the LGBTQIA community. Heterosexuals are not attacking homosexuals without being punished for it. What is happening is that heterophobia is rampant and the LGBTQIA community is attacking heterosexuality. Now the situation is reversed and it's the LGBTQIA community who are not being punished. This is why the heterosexual community has to take a stand, not physically, insisting on our right to freedom of speech and the right to remain heterosexual.

Heterosexuals, you don't owe homosexuals anything. Why do I say this? Because their heterophobia is being led by a desire for revenge, control, and power as they seek to execute a hostile takeover of US society.

The LGBTQIA community is fighting dirty against heterosexuals. They will do whatever it takes to gain power and control over heterosexuals, including lying, manufacturing outrage, and getting heterosexuals fired from any job or canceled from any platform that gives them a voice to tell their side of the story, at the same time silencing or censoring the voices of heterosexuals and bullying them into the closet. This erasing of heterosexuality has to be exposed and addressed. The LGBTQIA community with its cancel culture is the alphabet's mob bullying tactic of choice. Heterosexuals, you are losing this fight.

This is how the LGBTQIA community is winning the war that they have waged upon you: by shutting down their opponents' voices and not letting them counterargue and share their points of view. Because the LGBTQIA community knows that it is not fighting fair, it won't allow the opposition an opportunity to exposed them, so instead they cancel the opposition by manufacturing outrage and claiming offensiveness and thereby getting authority figures on their side to do their dirty work for them! This is a classic tactic called the sympathetic bully, which in this case involves canceling heterosexuals and bullying them into the closet.

Chapter 11

Groupthink or a Cult?— Acceptance Over Freedom

Tyranny of the minority—a culture of oppression and harsh and unjust acts.

The LGBTQIA community does not get to ram their identity or ideology down our throats and bully heterosexuals into the closet. We get to decide our own identity and beliefs.

Some people would rather have their personal freedom of speech taken away from them in exchange for being liked and accepted. Such people prefer not to think for themselves and to fall in line with the group, rather than being their own person, thinking on their own, valuing their individuality, or go things alone. Why? Because there is safety and strength in numbers. However, this is a double edge sword. Groupthink, which is rampant among the LGBTQIA community, is very dangerous as it is how hostile mobs and cults are formed. A cult will shape the minds of weak loners who want to fit in, brainwashing them with lies and get them to do things that go against their own best interests. This is exactly what happens to most members of the LGBTQIA community. The leaders of the LGBTQIA community have exploited the weaknesses of individuals and have convinced them by way of indoctrination and brainwashing that they are victims of offensive homophobia and bullying abuse from the heterosexual community as a whole. The LGBTQIA community has persuaded these individuals to believe that if anyone opposes them, disagrees with them, or questions them, then that person is homophobic, rather than raising a simple point of disagreement. This is why groupthink is dangerous, because people who engage in it do not think for themselves. Instead, the LGBTQIA community is turning its members into a force of so-called "victims," and they will eventually cause these individuals to go on the offensive and start being heterophobic, hating and attacking anything heterosexual.

This is similar to how Jim Jones and Charles Manson each formed a cult and got their followers to attack and kill innocent people such as the Tates and the LaBiancas in California. Jim Jones was an infamous cult leader who in the seventies got his members to give up their individuality and engage in groupthink, following him into a mass suicide by drinking Kool-Aid laced with poison. This is where the famous phrase comes from, "Don't drink the Kool-Aid," meaning do not buy the lie, because if you do, then you will be led astray. As far as Charles Manson goes, he directed a group of members of his cult to go and kill the famous Hollywood families called Tate and LaBianca. He got female loners hooked on drugs and then over time led them astray to commit murder. This happened in the sixties. Ironically, one of the members, Leslie Van Houten, just got paroled this year (2023). She had been in prison for more than fifty years. Charles Manson died in prison.

I'm *not* comparing LGBTQIA members to Jim Jones's or Charles Manson's demonic behavior, but I am comparing groupthink to cultlike behavior. People who engage in groupthink are followers and will fall in line with whatever the leaders tell them to do. They have given up their individuality and their own ways of thinking. The weak-minded, loners, losers, misfits, and people looking to fit in with a group are more susceptible to engage in groupthink. They are easily persuadable, meaning that they will fall into line with whatever the leaders tell them to do, even if it goes against their own best interests. These are the same kind of people whom Jim Jones and Charles Manson attracted and the same MO each of them used: gather the weak-minded, the loners, and the people who want to fit in with crowd and get them to groupthink, then you can control their every thought and make them do as you tell them, even if it will hurt them in the process. That's why groupthink is like cultish behavior, because it has the same MO. Therefore, the comparison I'm making concerns the MO, which in this case is groupthink, of cult leaders Charles Manson or Jim Jones, and not any similarity between these two men and the LGBTQIA community.

That said, groupthink is behind the alphabet mob's being sent out like an attack dog. Half the time when you ask these LGBTQIA attackers what or whom they are opposing, why, and what the issues are, they can't tell you. Why? Because they just follow the orders of their LGBTQIA leaders. Just like a cult member would. Groupthink is the gateway to becoming a cult member. Why do I say this? Because the MOs are exactly the same. Now the LGBTQIA community will turn heterophobic and try to attack and erase anything and everything having to do with heterosexuality. This is what we see in today's society, an LGBTQIA community that has gone unchallenged and unchecked by the heterosexual community. Many LGBTQIA community leaders are intentionally leading weak-minded loners and people who are susceptible to groupthink to become heterophobic in our society. Then these same LGBTQIA leaders, who have engaged in heterophobia or have become heterophobic themselves, try to turn the tables on heterosexuals and make it appear as if they are the victims of homophobia. Why? Remember, they have conditioned the members of the LGBTQIA community, through groupthink, to believe that they can do no wrong, that they are victims, and that it's the fault of heterosexuals because they opposed them, challenged them, or questioned them.

Those LGBTQIA members who went out and spit on people and threw objects at Riley Gaines and the others did so because they were told to. I say this with confidence because certainly someone had to tell them that the ceremony was to take place on that day and at that time. These people could have easily gone to jail, and should've gone to jail, for assault, which would have gone against their own best interests. All because they engaged in groupthink. This is why groupthink is like cultish behavior, and is very dangerous. Because what those LGBTQIA members did was only one or two steps away from murder. Those objects they were throwing could have hit one of those kids in the head, in some kind of freak accident, and killed them. Which again would go against their own best interests, as they were sent out to attack heterosexuals on behalf of the LGBTQIA community, a.k.a. the alphabet mob.

Chapter 12

LGBTQIA—"Erasing" Biological Women in Sports and Replacing Them with the LGBTQIA Version of a Woman, That Is, Trans Women, a.k.a. Biological Males: Why the Feminists and the #MeToo Movement Will Not Defend Biological Women's Sports

Tyranny of the minority—a culture of oppression and harsh and unjust acts.

The LGBTQIA community does not get to ram their identity or ideology down our throats and bully heterosexuals into the closet. We get to decide our own identity and beliefs.

Fifty percent of the responsibility for this problem falls directly at the feet of the feminist movement, and responsibility for the other 50 percent falls at the feet of the LGBTQIA community. What do I mean? The feminists have been trying to make the point that men and women are equal in every way, including athletic ability. The feminists have gotten women to challenge men at every turn and to dismiss the biological differences between the genders. They have gotten women to break apart men-only golf clubs and boys-only Boy Scouts by allowing women or girls to join. They have gotten women to enlist in the military and serve in combat, which used to be reserved for men only. It all started with the famous tennis match between Billie Jean King and Bobby Riggs, to which King, a gay woman, was challenged by Riggs, a heterosexual man, and she won. However, note that she was a professional tennis player and that he was just an average middle-aged man at the time. Regardless, this event is where the feminists got the idea for women to challenge men in sports. After the feminists and members of women's groups decided they wanted to advance their careers and started challenging men in the workplace, they became overconfident and invited themselves into men's sports. Women today have been brainwashed by the feminists into believing the foolish theory that women are equal to men in athletic ability. Yes, I said foolish.

This situation has set women up for failure. See, the feminists have a plan to take men down and gain power for themselves. I wrote a book on this topic called *Millennium Women and Gender Assassination: The Plot to Destroy All Things Male*. Feminists believe if they just get women to say that they are equal to men, then that's case closed: it means that they are equal, which is totally not so. Why do I say this? Because equality has to be proven, not just spoken into existence. The feminists forgot to prove that women are equal to men in all ways, and therein lies the problem. See, as long as the feminists can just say or get other women to just say that they are equal to men, then they can call men sexist or misogynistic, and the men will let them win or have their way. Remember, this can only stand as long as the women don't have to prove that they are equal to men. Everyone knows that men and women are not equal biologically. Now are there exceptions to the rules? Sure there are. However, the rules are still the rules.

Let's compare women saying they are equal to me to me getting into the boxing ring with Mike Tyson in his prime. As long as I can talk a good game and say that I'm equal to him *without proving it*, then I am equal in everyone's eyes. And that is the theory behind women's advancement movement and the feminist push for gender equality in sports. Just saying women are equal but not having to prove it is the way to gain power and control over men. That's one way (not every way) that the feminist movement has empowered women over men. It's a con game. Now if any man opposes this theory, he will be smeared, publicly shamed, and canceled and thereby deemed as sexist and misogynistic. That's one way (not every way) the feminists have empowered women over men. Herein lies the problem. They failed to account for the transgender female, that is, the biological male claiming to be a woman. So here comes the real challenge, because now the feminists have to put up or shut up and prove what they have been saying, that women are equal to men in athletic ability.

Remember my analogy of me getting into the boxing ring with Mike Tyson in his prime? I've talked a good game, but now I have to put up and prove that I can hold my own or shut up. Well, that's where women are today. Talk is cheap. Now it's time for action. Now that the feminists, the women's groups, and women themselves have to prove that they are equal, they can't measure up. The problem is that they never could measure up to men in terms of strength and size. The feminists, like the LGBTQIA community, used intimidation and bullying tactics against men to strongarm their way into power. Now that certain biologically male members of the LGBTQIA community have seen this weakness in women's sports, they have exploited it, because it was the feminists and the women themselves who invited the LGBTQIA community and the trans female, who is a biological male, into women's sports to compete with them in a head-to-head battle. Why? Because the women themselves said that they were equal to men in athletic ability.

It all backfired. Let's take the example of transgender swimmer Lia Thomas. This is a biological male who was a mediocre swimmer in the men's field. He then turned transgender and entered women's swimming, where he started competing with women. His performance far exceeded that of every woman on the swim team, and he broke almost every record. He took awards and prize money that otherwise would have been awarded to biological women. And now the same women who insisted they were equal to men in athletic ability are now complaining that this is unfair to them and that this man shouldn't be allowed to compete in women sports. Now I feel conflicted here because I don't believe that this man should be in women's sports either. However, it was the feminists and the women's groups who invited him in with their false belief that they were equal to men in every way, including athletic ability. Now it is these same feminist women who want the very same men to take the lead and get this man and other men out of their sport because they can't measure up as they claimed to have been able. When men were trying to warn women about was that this was not a good idea and that they are unable to measure up to men's strength, these very same women called them sexist and misogynistic and tried to bully them, intimidate them, and get them canceled. Now they want these same men, whom they shamed and smeared as sexist and misogynistic, to help them.

I've got a question. Where are the feminists? How come they

aren't helping these women? Where is the protest, the outrage? Where are the women's marches to bring attention to this issue? I'll tell you why there is no protest and no outrage from among the feminists: because most feminists in positions of leadership are gay or otherwise members of the LGBTQIA community. You have to know the history of the feminist movement, how it started and who started it.

The feminist movement started in the late sixties and early seventies, and guess by whom? Gay women, transgender people, and female men-haters! Those women are in their sixties and seventies today—the Billie Jean Kings, Hillary Clintons, Oprah Winfreys, and Randi Weingartens of the world. In other words, they are still alive, leading the women's movement and the feminist movement, and at the same time some of them are leading the LGBTQIA community. Get it now? How do you expect them to go against their own interests? The LGBTQIA /feminist movement initially used straight women to help them advance their cause to take the power away from men and give it to themselves. They tricked heterosexual women into merging with them and fighting their cause, and now that they have the power and protected class status of the LGBTQIA community, they no longer have any use for straight women, so they are throwing them under the bus. This is why you don't see any organized women's movement or protests, because some of the feminists and some of the leaders of the LGBTQIA community *are the same people.*

Take soccer player Megan Rapinoe, who has come out in favor of transgenders. Why? Because she is gay and a member of the LGBTQIA community. She sees biological women as the enemy now that she is retired and therefore doesn't have to face transgender females, that is, biological males, in a head-to-head competition. However, the salient point is that the transgenders are her people, *not the straight heterosexual women.* Get it now? She has no use for straight women.

They can be canceled or erased for all she cares. Remember, this is the goal of the LGBTQIA community, to erase heterosexuality. Don't believe me? Then explain why the feminists who are also leaders of the LGBTQIA community won't help heterosexual women. Explain why gay woman Megan Rapinoe will not vouch for women's rights. It's because straight women get in the way of the rights of the LGBTQIA community, so they must be erased. Heterosexual women, you'd better wake up, because the LGBTQIA community has waged war on you. That's why they refuse to define what a woman is.

It's because they want their version of a woman to be the standard. Guess who that woman is? You got it: the transgender woman, that is, a biological male, the very same "woman" you want out of your sport. Checkmate: you have just been erased! However, if you try to challenge transgender women, they are going to send the alphabet mob after you and call you a homophobe and try to cancel you. Get it now? My suggestion for heterosexual women is to push back now before you become extinct. I don't know how much more proof you need that the LGBTQIA community is planning a hostile takeover of society and that they are starting with the erasing of straight women. Their endgame is to totally erase heterosexuality from the planet. You don't have to believe me: just look at the schools, the advertising, and society itself, and you'll see the evidence everywhere. However, if you still don't believe me, then just sit back and watch as you become a second-class citizen behind the LGBTQIA community while they dictate to you what your life choices will be. Watch as heterosexual women are erased from existence. Good luck!

Chapter 13

Social Media—the Alphabet Mob's Weapon of Choice

What role does social media play in the LGBTQIA community which causes this mob-like mentality? Millions of people are on social media, be it Facebook, Twitter or X, YouTube, Instagram, or some other platform, of which there are many. There are two full generations of people now who grew up using social media. In fact, that's all millennials and Generation Z'ers and know when it comes to communication. Few among them can function without it. I think there would be a sharp increase in the suicide rate if millennials and Generation Z'ers were deplatformed from social media sites, as they are literally addicted to them as if they were crack cocaine. As I'm writing about this on July 25, 2023, there are more than two hundred schools suing social media giants Facebook, Instagram, Google, YouTube, TikTok, and Snapchat for being harmful toward students.

Why are these social media platforms so dangerous for children? Because they are poisoning their young, impressionable minds, teaching them negative behavior, and steering them toward what the social media platforms want them to focus their attention on and not necessarily on what the young people want. If these social media giants want their younger users to follow a so-called trending topic, they'll add it as a choice to their search engine results. At that point the users are a captive audience, meaning that they have no choice but to focus on what the social media platform has put in front of them. These social media platforms are only interested in making money off as many users as they can. However, they know that they can use a psychological angle to lure in young, impressionable children and entangle them in a web of darkness, which will only help the social media platforms make more profit from the data. However, this practice goes against the children's best interests.

Now let's look at this issue from the LGBTQIA community's perspective. Social media is the perfect place for a bullying platform. Literally. People can voice their opinions and vent their disrespect and hate at the same time. Now I'm a free speech person. I believe that everyone should have the opportunity to state their own opinions, even if other people don't like the opinions or even if they are wrong. Remember, with the First Amendment and freedom of speech, you also have the right to be wrong. There is no such thing as misinformation or disinformation. It's called your own opinion. Freedom of speech is intended to protect the speech that people disagree with or don't like. If you who don't agree and you believe that people should be silenced and censored for their opinions, who are you to tell me and others what we can and cannot say? Who put you in charge of the rest of us? Who made you the ultimate authority figure over us? Nobody! Remember, if you get to tell me what I can and can't say, then I also get to tell you what you can and can't say. So I guess nobody will be able to voice their own opinions anymore. Now what kind of country are we going to have, an authoritative dictatorship? The United States of America would be over as we know it. That leads me to ask, why does the LGBTQIA community believe that they can say hateful things to heterosexuals but that heterosexuals don't have the right to say hateful things to them? Why is the LGBTQIA community protected, but the heterosexual community is not protected from the LGBTQIA community? It's hypocrisy and a double standard that has to stop! This is why I wrote *The LGBTQIA Community and Betrayal*, because heterophobia is real, and many (not all) in the LGBTQIA community engage in it all the time.

Many (not all) members of the LGBTQIA community will try to get any and all heterosexuals off social media platforms if they feel offended by them. However, they are the ones who get to determine what's offensive or not. Something doesn't have to actually be offensive toward the LGBTQIA community, it's just that someone from that community has to feel it is offensive. However, if a person from the heterosexual community tries to get a LGBTQIA community person canceled from a social media platform for how he or she has been made to feel, then it's the person from the heterosexual community who will be deemed as homophobic or offensive for the so-called "attack" on an LGBTQIA community member. Do you see anything wrong with this picture? I do. It means the LGBTQIA community can do no wrong and can say whatever they want to heterosexuals, but heterosexuals can't even defend themselves against the LGBTQIA community without being called homophobic. This is a double standard that has put heterosexuals into a subordinate role where they have to be subservient to the LGBTQIA community. That's BS! It's a clever con game by some (not all) members of the LGBTQIA community, the purpose being to get and maintain power and control over the heterosexual community and, in this case, bully them into the closet and erase them from society.

Social media has paved the way for our communication today. It's the way we get our message across to the masses. However, if only one voice, that of the LGBTQIA community, can be heard, then that community will deem any speech of the heterosexual community that they don't like or just disagree with as hate speech. That makes them heterophobic according to their own logic. They can say that anything is offensive to them, even if it's not meant that way, and get some heterosexual person deplatformed, which puts too much power and control in the wrong person's hands, which can destroy another person's livelihood or life without due process. On social media I can find page after page of LGBTQIA community members using hateful speech against heterosexuals that hasn't been removed, but I can't find any hateful speech against the LGBTQIA community that's still posted. Any such posts will be taken down immediately, and that person who put up the post will be deplatformed. See anything wrong with that? I do. Social media has given many (not all) in the LGBTQIA community the opportunity to bully heterosexuals at will, which is heterophobic. Most LGBTQIA millennials and Generation Z'ers get their news from social media. Social media is also how they get their own personal messages out. So social media is the bully pulpit for LGBTQIA community members to shut down and erase heterosexuality. If heterosexuals can't get their messages out to those two generations and balance out the false claims made by some (not all) in the LGBTQIA community, then the LGBTQIA community will have erased the voices of truth from the heterosexual community without due process.

There is a saying, "If an accusation that goes unchallenged, then it's considered to be true." This is how many (not all) in the LGBTQIA community have been able to erase the many viewpoints and voices of the heterosexual community. This is how many (not all) in the LGBTQIA community operate. They want to cancel heterosexuals and prohibit their messages from being heard by getting them deplatformed. Also, they scream, yell, and shout down heterosexual speakers so that their voices literally can't be heard on college campuses when they come to visit and want to tell their stories or get their messages across to the people who invited them. Therefore, there is nothing to post on social media because the speeches could not be heard. That's in the LGBTQIA playbook for erasing heterosexuality from our society.

This means that now the LGBTQIA community can get their accomplish their agenda without any opposition or pushback from the heterosexual community. And this is why there are drag queen strip shows, why homosexuality is taught to children through children books, and why not students in grade schools aren't allowed to tell their parents about these things, keeping secrets from their own parents who are responsible for them. This is also the reason why more than two hundred schools are suing social media platforms for harming our young, innocent, and very impressionable children. This so-called "protected class" has been emboldened to bully, harass, discriminate against, and erase the heterosexual community whenever they feel offended. How? By keeping the people uninformed and uneducated, at which point you can tell them a one-sided story and they will believe it because they have nothing else to counter it with. No checks. This is why many (not all) in the LGBTQIA community promote censorship. And most of the social media platforms are leftist and go along with the LGBTQIA community, a.k.a. the alphabet mob.

Chapter 14

The LGBTQIA Movement and Climate Change—Real or a Hoax?

The problem is not climate change; it's fuel change. Climate change is the biggest scam in history, with its purpose being to control the energy. Whoever controls the energy dominates the world. Climate change is a hoax!

If the government and politicians can change the weather, then why haven't so far with the billions and trillions of dollars that they have spent on green energy to slow climate change? When are the hurricanes going to stop? When are the glaciers going to stop melting? When are the heat waves going to subside? When are the snowstorms going to slow down? When are the tornadoes and the mudslides going to stop? Oh yeah, I forgot that humankind can't control or change the weather. So, the government and the leftist politicians are just stealing our money through the kickbacks they are getting from proponents of this so-called "green energy" policy that they are subsidizing, and they keeping going back for more.

It's a hoax. Climate change is all the government and the leftists, including the LGBTQIA community, want to talk about. Why is our government pushing climate change and expecting the LGBTQIA community to blindly support this cause? I'll tell you why. The LGBTQIA community is part of the so-called "protected class." Why would the government want to back and protect the LGBTQIA community without anything in return? There is no such thing as something for nothing. There is a saying, "If you scratch my back, I'll scratch yours." In other words, I'll protect you if you support me. So what the government has done is to have given the LGBTQIA community a free pass to do whatever they please, including bully heterosexuals, by having passed laws to protect them, in exchange for their support on climate change and other issues that they want votes for. Now whatever the leftist politicians want from this group, they will get it from the LGBTQIA community and any other community they want. This includes their being sent out like the mob or an attack dog to bully people, protest certain activities or ideas, and shut down anyone who mounts opposition to their agenda, which includes abortion and climate change. Now the government and the leftists have an in-house bully attack machine that they can "secretly" send out at will to protect the leftist agenda without taking responsibility for these groups' behaviors. It's called "plausible deniability." In other words, they can play dumb or pretend as if they don't know who or what these people are, that they don't know anything about it. It's the same thing that they did in the summer of 2020 before the presidential election with the group Black Lives Matter. This was a well-funded and coordinated attack on the major cities in the country to keep the economy shut down to make it appear as if things were going to hell so that the government could come in like a knight in shining armor and fix them. The leftists intentionally broke the economy by shutting down businesses with violence, and then claimed that they could fix it. That's why most all the leftist politicians in the major cities allowed the so-called "peaceful protesters" to destroy their cities by rioting and looting without any law enforcement resistance. The police were told to stand down by the mayors and governors of the Democratic cities and states. Why? Because the politicians wanted to let the rioters do the job of tearing down the economy and putting fear into the voters so that they could win the election based on the economy. Don't believe it? Then explain why the politicians allowed this travesty to happen in our society. Barring that, I'll tell you why: *politics.* It was the same thing with the COVID-19 fears. Anytime that anyone questioned or opposed the COVID-19 mandates, the government and the leftist politicians sent out the so-called "peaceful protesters," who were really the bully mob, to intimidate and shut down the opposition, even if they had a valid point, because it got in the way of their agenda. The government and the leftist politicians are using these groups as a political pawn to bully people in an elaborate scam to intimidate the American people and force them into submission. That also includes the LGBTQIA community, whom the government protects and treats like royalty because the leftist politicians want something in exchange for protecting them. There is no such thing as something for nothing, so their mob-like protection has a price. Climate change is a scam and a hoax. However, the government needs the American people to get behind this hoax, because it's not about the climate, it's about the fuel and energy. There is no such thing as "man-made" climate change; it's called nature! Human beings can't control the weather even if they wanted to.

Still, climate change is the snake oil that the government is selling the American people and the world. The Far Left Democrats understand that they have a group of voters who will believe anything that they tell them no matter what because they know that the Left-leaning news media, including social media, will reinforce their point of view even though it's a lie and a total hoax.

Why is climate change a lie and a hoax? I'll tell you why. The government is telling people that we need to lower carbon emissions and make the transition from fossil fuels to electricity, including electricity to power cars, to arrest climate change. OK, that sounds good, but what's wrong with it? Nothing if it works. But it does not work. If the issue is climate change and not fuel change, then tell me how does going electric and using wind and solar power stop the hurricanes, wildfires, and tornadoes, and stop the glaciers from melting? The government tells you the problem and gives the answer, then nothing happens. But the same thing has been going on for centuries, meaning natural events. We had category 5 hurricanes before cars, planes, and trains were even invented. What caused those extreme weather events? It wasn't cars, which operate on gas and oil, because gas and oil weren't around at that time?

The weather changes every year like clockwork, but now the government and half the paid scientists are saying that it's all from too much carbon in the atmosphere with no proof from the other half of the scientific community to back up this claim. The other half of the scientific community (the ones who are censored and to whom the mainstream media will give no airtime) say that there is no scientific proof that climate change is man-made, meaning it's a hoax. This is why I say it's a lie. Because we never hear the government say (with facts and data to back up their climate change theory) what the endgame is. How much do we have to sacrifice in order to get emissions down? By how much do we need to lower emissions? And how much money is this going to cost us? And if we succeed, is it going to lower the number of hurricanes, snowstorms, wildfires, etc.? Those are key points to know if you really want the climate to change, right? Let me ask all the climate change believers some questions: Where is the emissions level at this point, and how much do we need to lower it by? How many electric cars do we have to buy in order to replace gasoline-powered cars? How much money will we have to spend on this effort?

I guarantee you that 99.9999 percent of climate change believers can't answer one of those questions? Why not? Because the same government and politicians who lied to us can't give us an answer that they don't have!

Why don't they have those answers? Because the answers don't exist. Why not? Because the government never intended for "green energy" to change the climate. They also never intended to be questioned about it. They thought that the American people should just fall in line, do as they're are told, and just blindly believe what they say. So tell me, how can they fix the problem of climate change if they can't even define the problem? The answer is that they can't! However, the government and politicians are out here every day preaching climate change and scaring the hell out of young people, leading them to believe that they are going to die in twelve years as espoused by Al Gore, John Kerry the so-called "climate czar," and Congressperson Alexandria Ocasio-Cortez (a.k.a. AOC), just to name a few. There are many others.

However, have you noticed that every time they mention climate change, they ask for money or try to get you to contribute to some big business car companies? What happened to all the money that the government printed and spent on so-called "green energy"? And why are they giving incentives for car companies if consumers are buying electric vehicles? What's in it for the car companies, and what's in it for the government, who partners with the car companies to get you to purchase these electric vehicles?

There's a saying: "Follow the money and you'll find the crime." I know some of the climate change believers are saying to themselves,

What crime? And who are the criminals? Well, I'll tell you what's the crime and who will profit or gain from these lies they have told you. First, the crime: lying to the American people and, under false pretenses, getting climate change believers to spend their money on electric vehicles and other so-called "green energy" products so car makers can make a profit off them with no intention of delivering the product that they sold them. The product in this case is reducing emissions so that we can have clean, healthier air. It's never going to happen the way that it was sold to the American people, because the government can't even tell us where the emissions level is at this time, or how much it will take to reduce it over what period of time if we buy electric vehicles rather than gasoline-powered cars.

Now the weather. The government can't tell you how climate change will change the weather. In other words, will there be fewer hurricanes and wildfires? Will the glaciers stop melting? Will the tornadoes, snowstorms, and massive heat waves slow down or stop? These are the things that the government brings up, telling the American people that they will stop *if* we just give them the money and provide our support to make it happen. However, the government can neither predict nor change the weather. But *they are taking your money and changing your habits and lifestyle*, all in the name of climate change. Also, if this were really about emissions and lowering them, then tell me how do you manufacture an electric battery, solar panels, and wind turbines without fossil fuels, which include coal, gas, and oil, the very same things that the government is telling the American people to stop using and get rid of and replace with electricity? You don't! So it makes no sense. And if it makes no sense, then *it's not true!*

Now let me tell you what climate change is really about. It's not climate change, it's fuel change! Humankind can't change the weather because humankind didn't create the weather. Only God can do that. However, humankind can change the fuel, because humankind drills and refines the fuel from the earth's natural resources. Remember, fuel is money, and those two together equal power. Whoever controls the fuel has the power, and that power and control runs the world. That's massive power.

Let's look at the war between Russia and Ukraine. Countries and wars are run on *energy*. Fuel runs the cars, trains, buses, tanks, planes, rockets, bombs, etc., so if a country like Russia invades a country like Ukraine, then whichever of the two has the most fuel and energy will win the war, conquering the other country.

This is the problem that the NATO countries had. They gave up their fossils fuel for so-called "green energy" and then turned to Russia, who is their enemy, for help with energy when their "green energy" proved to be not enough or *didn't work*! Well, that was a major mistake, relying on the enemy to help them fuel their country. Now that Russia has invaded Ukraine, the NATO countries are at Russia's mercy. Now Russia can dictate to them and manipulate their energy supply or take over their country. Remember, after World War II, NATO was created to stop the Soviet Union, which is Russia today, from taking over the world by force. Now look at how foolish NATO is to depend on the enemy to fuel its members countries. Now the United States is in the same situation as the NATO countries are in, but our enemy is China. China wants to replace the United States as the number one superpower in the world. They have built the most powerful navy, even more powerful than that belonging to the United States. They have built hypersonic weapons. We don't have any hypersonic weapons at this time. They are preparing for war with the United States, and we are neither ready nor prepared.

Now let's take a look at our green energy policy. We are trying to transition our vehicles from gas powered to electric. Now to all those who believe in climate change, I have a question for you. Where do you think we get the batteries for the vehicles once we change over and strip our energy resources down to nothing? What country makes batteries, wind turbines, and solar panels? You guessed it: China, the enemy of the United States, the very same country that wants to take us down as the number one superpower and destroy us. This has to be the dumbest thing that we could ever do as a country. We are following in NATO's foolish footsteps. Also, climate change is one of the largest scams in the world. Before I go deeper into why it's a scam and a hoax, first let me tell you the true story of how buses came about for us to ride on (i.e., mass transportation). Back in the early 1900s, this country's primary form of mass transportation was the trolley.

Trolleys took us from work to home, to stores for shopping, and wherever else we wanted to go, just like today's buses. Then one day an anonymous individual started to buy up the trolleys one by one, and then this person started to replace the trolleys with buses, until the majority of trolleys were gone from the streets. Then the local government tracked down this anonymous person's identity and took the person to court for being a fraud and a scam. However, by the time that government had won its case against the scammer and con artist, it was too late because most of the trolleys had been disposed of and were replaced by buses. So buses were the new form of mass transportation in the United States.

What does this story have to do with climate change? I'll tell you: climate change is a scam and a fraud put forth by the government and the Far Left in order to change the *fuel or energy and not the weather*. Humankind can't change the weather no matter what you've been told. And by the time the climate change believers find out that it is a scam, a lie, and a hoax and that humankind really can't change the weather, it will be too late and we will have changed all our energy and fuel to electric, solar, and wind. And then we will be dependent on our enemy, China, for our energy resources, who will manufacture a war that will destroy the United States because of our energy dependency and deprivation. Then we will be looking back just like the NATO countries and be at the mercy of our enemy. Then all the climate change believers will be upset that they got tricked and were lied to. However, it was their complicity that destroyed our nation. Because people blindly believed the government's lies and didn't look deep enough or question the government and the Far Left politicians who are hoaxers and scammers, such as AOC, Al Gore, and John Kerry. What I'm saying here is common sense. Ask the government who fed you all these lies.

I have a question. If human beings are able to change the climate and the weather, then how are we going to do it? How can we stop a hurricane? How we stop a wildfire? How can we stop mudslides? How can we stop tornadoes? How can we stop the glaciers from melting? How can we stop snowstorms? All from just lowering our carbon emissions? *No!* Because that's not what causes these weather events to happen in the first place. It's nature, natural events that happen every year to keep planet Earth in line with the rest of our solar system. However, the government has used climate change as a vehicle to take our hard-earned tax dollars and spend them on its own selfish pursuits, transitioning from fossil fuels to so-called "green energy" with the intended change, which is weather control, never coming about. That is what makes this a hoax!

We in the United States have given trillions of dollars to the climate change cause. Ask yourself these questions: where is the money, what did it go toward, who got paid, why are they asking for more money even though they can't tell us where the money is or what was it spent on, and what is the progress of emissions control? This story sounds kind of funny. It kind of sounds like a big lie! That's because it is. Al Gore, a climate change fanatic, has been saying for twenty-plus years that the world will have boiling oceans. I'm still waiting on my hot tub, Al. Where is it? AOC said that the world is going to end in twelve years, and that was four years ago. I guess we have only eight years left on the planet. Better start living it up and spending every day as if it's your last. Greta Thunberg, a thirteen-year-old child at the time she made her worldwide speech on climate change, made it clear that we all are in danger if we don't fix the planet now. I'm sure with her wealth of knowledge, she has great vision and psychological experience to predict the future at the grand old age of thirteen. Oh yeah, she was fed the speech by someone else and was told what to say.

There are people who literally make life-or-death decisions based on climate change. Some people are choosing not to have children because they have bought into the lie that the world is going to end in twelve years as AOC had said, or because Al Gore has told them the oceans will be soon boiling—just crazy things that don't make any sense. Climate change believers have drunk the Kool-Aid and bought the snake oil from these opportunistic politicians who just want their votes. As for me and anyone else who has common sense, when it comes to climate change, I believe one person and one person only, and that's God. Why God? Because God made a promise to humankind that he would never flood or destroy the earth again, and the sign of his promise was a rainbow. He said, "This is a reminder of my promise. I will never again destroy the earth."

I have set my rainbow in the clouds, and it will be
the sign of the covenant between me and the earth.
Whenever I bring clouds over the earth and the
rainbow appears in the clouds, I will remember my
covenant between me and you and all living creatures
of every kind. Never again will the waters become
a flood to destroy all life. Whenever the rainbow
appears in the clouds, I will see it and remember
the everlasting covenant between God and all living
creatures of every kind on the earth. (Genesis 9:13–16)

Case closed!

Chapter 15

Being Gay—Born That Way or a Choice?

I have heard many people say that they were "born that way," meaning gay. They say that it's not a choice. I believe that both possibilities— being born gay and choosing to be gay—are right at the same time. What do I mean? I believe that some gay people are born that way, and at the same time I believe that some people choose to be gay. You are likely thinking, *How in the hell is that possible? It has to be one or the other.* Actually it doesn't. To me, being born gay is like having sexual dyslexia. What do I mean? Gay people view their sex or gender as backward. A gay man feels female but has male body parts. I believe that somewhere in the development stages when the child's brain was forming and its body was developing, the gender developed opposite to the brain, meaning the brain went female and the body went male, or vice versa. You may be asking, "How is that possible? You don't know; you're not a doctor or a scientist. You're just making things up." I may not be a doctor or a scientist, but there is one thing I do know, and it's that all babies' bodies start off as female, then the brain starts developing the sexual parts of the body. Sometimes the Y chromosome goes one way and the X chromosome goes the other way in terms of gender: the body and the brain go in totally opposite directions. Now you may be saying to yourself, *How do you know that all babies start off as female?* There is a one thing on a man's body that shows that this is the case: *nipples*. Men have nipples. Why? There is no biological function for them.

What's a nipple? A nipple is a dormant breast. The breast has one function and one function only: to produce milk to feed a baby. So why do men have nipples if they can't breastfeed? It's because all babies start with the intent of being female. Then the developmental process happens, and when the baby's body goes to develop nipples, if the baby is going in the male direction, then the nipples are stifled and go dormant, whereas female nipples continue to develop for the purposes of breastfeeding.

What if something goes wrong in the developmental process at the exact moment when the baby is going to go male or female? What if the woman smokes, drinks alcohol, or does drugs while she is pregnant? I'm not saying that these situations would cause these particular birth defects in these cases, or that they might cause a baby to be born gay. Don't misinterpret or misunderstand me. I'm saying that this could be an explanation for why the body of a baby goes male and the mind or brain of that same baby goes female. There is no scientific theory for how or why babies are born gay. My explanation is one possibility for why a child would be born gay. Now before the PC or political correctness police get all hyped up and claim that this is supposedly offensive, allow me to say that nothing I'm saying is scientific or fact based. It's a theory for the sake of debate.

However, it is a logical theory that is more than likely right. We don't know, because everyone, including the scientific community, are too afraid of being attacked by the alphabet mob to come out with a study like this. However, for scientific reasons, a study like this should be done. I bring this theory up because if turning gay is a birth defect, then why aren't doctors or scientists trying to come up with a cure or solution? We try to fix every other mental illness except the gay illness. I know, right now you're likely saying, "You said that gay people have an illness and are mentally defective. It's offensive." This is a typical comment straight from the playbook of those who want to shut down any debate that they don't like as if the rest of us can't state our side of the story or our own opinions. The LGBTQIA community want only their opinions heard. That's the "sympathetic bully" tactic in full effect. It's not going to work here with me. I know the censor game, and I'm not playing it. Now back to the theory. Is this theory controversial? Sure it is. However, every scientific study or theory is controversial until it becomes a proven fact.

Name one study that had to do with the brain or sexual orientation that wasn't controversial. There is no such thing as a noncontroversial study when it comes to sexual orientation. Now I bring up this theory because there are a lot of gay people who don't want to be gay. They want some help to fix their unwanted problem. And yes, I say problem because it is a problem or a burden to these particular people. It may not be your individual problem as a member of the LGBTQIA community, but it is theirs, and you don't get to decide for them. We all are different in our thinking and tolerance level, so speak for yourself and not for others.

Especially refrain from speaking for the people who want real help. Now I say they want help because there is an entire group from the LGBTQIA community who wants that help—the T's. The transgender group are silently screaming from the rooftops about their condition, to the point where they are willing to take drastic action. What do I mean? Many (not all) transgender people will have permanent body-altering surgery to fix the gay problem that they believe they have. They believe that they were born in the wrong body. Don't believe it? If this is not the case, then explain why such a person who is biologically male but who feels female would have surgery to have his penis cut off and replaced with a vagina and then get into a relationship or marriage with a heterosexual man, and then go on to have a heterosexual relationship, not a homosexual relationship? So these transgender people really don't want to be gay. However, there are others in the LGBTQIA community who don't want transgender people to have sex-change operations because it takes away numbers from the gay community and puts those people in the heterosexual column.

Remember, there is strength in numbers, and gender reassignment subtracts from the LGBTQIA community's numbers. You may be thinking that people who have undergone gender reassignment surgery are still apart of the LGBTQIA community. That's only if they want to reveal their identity. Many don't want to be a part of that group. This is where the alphabet mob will try to bully them out of the closet—that is, stage a forced outing—just because they want these individuals on their side and with their group and against the heterosexual community. This is total selfishness and disrespect of individuals' wishes.

Many in the alphabet mob don't care about individuality. They just want what makes the group happy, and that's so-called "groupthink," which leads to bullying.

Anyway, that is my reasoning for why I believe that some people are born that way (i.e., gay). You may have a different theory, and that's OK. We all are entitled to our own opinions and I'm entitled to mine.

Let's take a look at my theory that being gay is a choice.

What makes a relationship a relationship? What makes a marriage a marriage? What makes a couple boyfriend and girlfriend? What makes a person gay or straight?

There is only one thing that makes relationships what they are, and that's sex. Having sex is the key to knowing what makes a relationship, a relationship. Without sex, the partners are just friends with feelings, each of them liking or loving the other. However, if a man claims that a woman he likes and is dating is his girlfriend but they have never had sex, is the woman really his girlfriend? I'm sure that 99.999 of women would say no. However, there is always that .000000001 remaining, the exception to the rule—basically insignificant. For all those who think that the exception it relevant, take your belief to a DNA court and try to get out of paying child support and see what the judge has to say. You may just find yourself going to jail, so don't do it!

Now if a couple gets married but they never consummate the marriage (meaning have sex), then are they legally married? In the eyes of the law, the answer is no.

If a same-sex, that is, gay, couple never have sex, are they really gay? The answer is no. They are just good friends who really like each other and have strong feelings for one another and just happen to be of the same gender or sex. Sex defines the relationship. So, without sex, you are not boyfriend and girlfriend, married or gay. It's like saying that you are a bank robber. You may feel that you can rob a bank, and you may have bank robbery tendencies, but until you commit the act of robbing a bank, then you're just a person with weird bank robbery feelings. *You are not a bank robber!* The same thing goes for murder. You may feel like murdering someone, but until you commit the act of murder, *you're not a murderer!* By the way, I'm *not* comparing being gay to being a killer or a bank robber. I'm comparing the act of sex as the defining thing that makes someone gay, and *not* his or her feelings or tendencies.

Now back to gay being a choice. If you claim to be gay, and if sex defines the relationship, then who put a gun to your head and made you put your penis in another man's anus? Nobody. That may sound graphic, but it describes what actually takes place. It was your choice as a man to become a gay man. You crossed the line voluntarily, meaning it was your choice to go to the other side and become gay. Therefore, anyone's being gay is their choice because they don't have to commit to a homosexual sexual act. A man doesn't have to have sex with another man. It is totally voluntary, 100 percent a choice.

Two men with homosexual leanings could easily restrain themselves, control their impulses, say no, and refrain from having gay sex, but they choose not to, which makes it their own personal, voluntary decision—a choice. Now some readers may be saying to themselves right now, *Who wants to go through life without having sex?* I understand that such a thing would be difficult. However there are plenty of virgins in the world, people who have never had sex. Sex is not guaranteed in life. It is also not an excuse to commit an homosexual act, which is the very thing that defines whether or not a person is gay. Many people say, "I'm gay because I was born that way." You were born with a certain mindset and with certain feelings, but these things don't make you gay. It is the *act of sex* that makes you gay, not your feelings or what you believe. You make a conscious, sound decision, and it is your own choice. Nobody forces you, putting a gun to your head and making you have gay sex. You *choose* it. Now with that being said, I don't care one way or the other if you are homosexual or heterosexual. I'm not going to harm you, hurt you, stop you from getting a job, a house, or anything, or stop you from marching in the pride parade. But I do disagree with you on this issue because I believe in God. So, your situation is between you and God or your Creator, not me. However, if the alphabet mob attacks me, then I will defend myself, my writings, and my work. I have a right to my opinions, and others who believe as I do have the same right to their opinions, just as you have a right to yours. We are all free and equal. As a human being, you are no better than me and I am no better than you. So, we may agree to disagree. Great debate.

Chapter 16

Is Being Gay like Being Black in the United States?

Why the LGBTQIA Community Tries to Merge Black and Gay Issues: Stealing the Pain of Black Slavery and Oppression to Advance the LGBTQIA Cause

Many people in the black community are saying of LGBTQIA people, "We gave them an inch, and they took a mile." The LGBTQIA community has used black people to advance themselves and secure protected class status. Every time the LGBTQIA community thought that they had been wronged or discriminated against, they used the phrase, "It's like being black." What does this mean? Black people were enslaved, oppressed, discriminated against, and persecuted like no other race or group of people in this country's history. And the LGBTQIA community has piggybacked on, hijacked, and stolen the pain of black people for use in their own cause, which is to gain power both in the LGBTQIA community and in our society, even over black people, the ones who have faced more persecution than anyone else in the United States. I don't recall any gay enslavement law in the United States. Now you may be saying that the LGBTQIA community and black Americans have undergone the same thing because they both have been discriminated against and subjected to some type of violence both. If so, you are partly right. However, many gay white people also discriminated against and committed violence against black people. Still in the closet, they were accepted by American society. However, some white gay discrimination against black people still exists to this day. I've seen it personally. A lot of white people who are gay and who are in powerful positions still discriminate against heterosexual black people when it comes to jobs, houses, bank loans, and other services and situations. Now if gay people were in the closet, they were still allowed to get jobs, buy houses, and exercise other rights and privileges they had as Americans without being discriminated against. Unlike black people. Black people were unable to hide their skin color, unlike gays, who could hide their homosexuality and therefore still benefited and thrived in the United States with no opposition or discrimination. So, the LGBTQIA argument that being gay is like being black is flawed and rooted in deception. The discrimination argument is not a real comparison when gay white people suffered no discrimination if they didn't tell people their sexual orientation. It's like when Bill Clinton, the former president of the United States, implemented the "Don't ask, don't tell" policy for the military. As long as you didn't tell anyone that you were gay, as a white male you were subjected to no discrimination. Now take the black military person. Black people were not allowed in the military simply because of their skin color. They couldn't use the protection law championed by Bill Clinton to save them from discrimination like the white gay person could. So to say that being gay is just like being black is just gay people stealing black people's pain and using it to advance their own causes. Why do I say this? Because gays weren't discriminated against like black people, and some white gay people were deeply involved in the discrimination against and hatred of black people, meaning they were committing hate crimes against heterosexual blacks just like their heterosexual white counterparts. They are still discriminating and committing hate crimes against black people to this day.

Also, gay people were not enslaved in the eyes of law and lynched and hung from trees like black people were. So it's disrespectful and disingenuous to compare the gay experience of discrimination and the black experience of discrimination and conclude they are the same. It's two totally different types of discrimination. Again, the LGBTQIA community stole the pain of black Americans and used it to advance their own cause and agenda, which is disingenuous. This practice is still going on to this day, whenever the LGBTQIA community can't stand on its own merits. Its members default to stealing black people's pain and using it to advance their cause. They say things like, "It's just like being black." That's in order to deflect attention from their cause and to put an end to the argument that they can't make it on their own merits. They try to make their argument better by using the black experience of pain because it was real and more intense.

My suggestion is for members of the LGBTQIA community to stand on their own feet and make their own point or debate it on its own merits and not use black people's history of pain and the merits of the black community. I say this because gay white people still discriminate against black people to this day! It's offensive and outrageous, and it must stop!

Chapter 17

Catholic Priests or Gay Pedophiles? Gay Predators in Priests' Clothing

For decades, the Catholic Church has been under scrutiny for child molestation. There is an image of priests as child molesters, with the narrative to match. However, everyone is afraid to address the elephant in the room because they don't want to be seen as homophobic. But the truth of the matter is that if we as a society want to truly protect children from sexual assault or molestation, then we have to take a look at it for what it really and truly is, which is gay pedophilia.

Many readers, especially those who are members of the LGBTQIA community, might say that the foregoing statement is homophobic. And therein lies the problem. Most (not all) members of the LGBTQIA community want to take any and all negative inferences about the LGBTQIA community and direct them onto other communities, as if they have no bad apples in their own community. I'm not saying *all* members of the LGBTQIA community are pedophiles, but I am saying that some bad apples from the LGBTQIA community are pedophiles—and we have to watch out for them. You may not like or agree with what I'm saying, and that's your prerogative, but it's doesn't detract from its possible truth. And to say otherwise defies logic.

I believe that priests who molest children are deceptive gay pedophiles who entered the priesthood under false pretenses specifically for that reason. There are gay pedophiles in schools. There are gay pedophiles in boys' clubs and Boy Scouts. There are gay pedophiles in day cares. There are gay pedophiles in every arena where children are accessible. So why wouldn't there be gay pedophiles in the Catholic Church? There are! Now in all the places where gay pedophiles exist, we don't demonize the schools, the Boy Scouts, or the day cares; we demonize the person or individuals who actually committed the crime. Only in the church do we blame it on the priests. Why? I'll tell you why. Because the LGBTQIA community is at war with the church. What do I mean by war with the church? For many gay people (although not all), the LGBTQIA community is their *church*. It's like any other denomination: Catholic, Jewish, Baptist, Protestant, LGBTQIA, et al. If you talk about religion, watch how people in the LGBTQIA community react or respond. They go into defense mode and start to oppose anything and everything about the church.

Why? It's because they have to justify their immoral behavior. Rather than acknowledge their sins, they defend their sins. We all sin, as human beings are not perfect. We all fall short of God's perfection. However, most of us will try to eradicate those sinful acts from our lives at some point. But if you don't acknowledge the sin or crime by deflecting it onto other people or communities, then how can you find the root of the problem and fix it? You can't. So, this pattern of pedophilia will continue with the abuse and harming of innocent children by the LGBTQIA community because it goes unacknowledged.

I pose a question to the LGBTQIA community: do you want to stop innocent children from being molested by some members of your community, or are you more concerned about your reputation?

Or is this part of the LGBTQIA community's war on the church, allowing the church or the priests to take the fall for gay pedophiles? The LGBTQIA community doesn't acknowledge that some of their own are pedophiles, and therefore they don't root out that evil. I say it's evil because children are being sexually and mentally abused with consequences that last a lifetime. That to me seems that the LGBTQIA community is at war with the church and religion. I know some readers may say that this is homophobic, which is a deflection. However, the LGBTQIA community still hasn't addressed the issue at hand. Are some Catholic priests gay pedophiles? The reason why I say gay pedophiles is because they seem to molest only little boys. Rarely do you ever hear of them molesting young girls. If at all.

I believe that some members of the LGBTQIA community, *not all*, are gay pedophiles. For purposes of illustration of my next point, let's take the priest aspect out of the conversation. If there was a child molester who sexually assaulted and abused only little boys in any other area or field of work, then what would we call him? A gay pedophile. Let's say that there is a child molester on the loose in the neighborhood who only molests young boys and we don't know who he is. Let's say that the FBI has to profile this person to find his MO. What would his profile be? How would the FBI describe the person to put out an APB (all-points bulletin)? I believe that the description would go like this: white male, early to midforties, possibly a child educator who has the job position, the opportunity, and the means to befriend young boys and is possibly gay. Why include gay in the description? Because if you put out a profile and omit the gay aspect, then there is a good chance that you may not catch this guy. Why not? Because it's a key piece of evidence that's crucial to the investigation. By leaving the gay aspect out, people would overlook some key spots where this guy may be hiding and the person whom he may be hanging around. So you would be going toward the east looking for a sunset, meaning that you would never find the perp. You would be taking investigators and the investigation toward countless dead ends with a good chance of wasting some countless amount of money and resources, which would make you a terrible investigator.

Now let's go back to the priest in the Catholic Church. If there is a child molester in the Catholic Church who is molesting young boys and we send in FBI agents who have been told by their supervisor that they can investigate everything except the gay aspect of the case, then tell me how they are going to find this person in a timely manner, before he sexually assaults or abuses another innocent child. The FBI would be putting themselves at a disadvantage if they were to buckle to their fear of what the LGBTQIA community thinks about what they are doing just because that community thinks that it is homophobia. My guess is, if you tie the hands of the investigators by making the investigation politically correct investigation and thereby overlooking the obvious clues, then there is a good chance that another child will be sexually abused or assaulted before the FBI finds the molester or pedophile. Therefore, by the LGBTQIA community's failure to be understanding and to take responsibility for one of their own bad apples, who is bringing great harm to innocent children, they contribute to the ability of child molesters to continue sexually abusing children. I ask a question to those who believe that this sort of situation is homophobic, because you don't want the LGBTQIA community to be blamed for the tragedy. Now I'm not blaming the LGBTQIA community for the acts of a pedophile, but I am blaming them for not allowing people to investigate the gay aspect of the perpetrator who is molesting these children. Some (not all) in the LGBTQIA community are more concerned about their image and reputation than they are about the actual child who is being sexually assaulted. That to me is disgusting and wrong!

Now to all those who don't want to look at the gay aspect of the description of the deceptive priest, actually a gay person pretending to be a priest, I ask you, are you willing to sacrifice your child and put him or her at risk of being sexually assaulted and mentally scarred for life because you turned a blind eye to the gay aspect of these so-called "priests," this because you were afraid of the alphabet mob coming after you and attacking you for being a homophobe or trying to cancel you from social media, or get you fired from your job, or do any other thing that they could do to destroy your life? If your answer is that you don't want to sacrifice your child but you are willing to sacrifice someone else's child, because you don't want to feel the wrath of the alphabet mob, then what kind of person does that make you? And what does that say about the LGBTQIA community? It says that they only give a damn about their own reputation and that your child can go to hell because they are better than you. It also says that your child means absolutely nothing and the LGBTQIA community means everything. That's why I call them the alphabet mob. They want to bully heterosexuals into the closet after they themselves have come out of the closet. Why? Because some (not all) want to take away our voices and opinions by canceling us, threatening us, silencing us, and censoring us. They do this to protect their own kind, and they'll use any means necessary, including sacrificing your innocent children to a gay pedophile, a deceptive, manipulative, and dishonest person parading around as a priest, hiding behind the cloth. For those who disagree with my opinions, findings, and conclusions, I say to you, if you turn a blind eye to the gay aspect, then you enable the continuing molestation of innocent children, especially young boys in the Catholic Church. I guess as long as it's someone else's children and not your own who are sacrificed, then it's OK, right? However, one day it just may be your innocent child who's, then you'll have no one to blame but yourself. We in this society have to scrutinize every group with a critical eye because there are bad people in every community, including the LGBTQIA community. The fact that the LGBTQIA community are given a pass in regard to the molestation of children by gay pedophiles says a lot about the power and influence they have on heterosexuals and the church itself.

We must not be afraid to the point that we, members of a civilized society, give the LGBTQIA community a free pass for allowing some of their own kind, in this case gay pedophiles, to sexually abuse our innocent children. Everyone guilty in the LGBTQIA community must be held accountable. They are no exception! No one is above scrutiny and criticism when what they're doing is negative! There are checks and balances on everything and everyone, and again the LGBTQIA community is no exception!

Why are some people afraid to call it what it is—which is gay pedophilia? Because the perpetrators molest only young, innocent boys and not girls. This means that these deceptive priests are gay. How can we as a society stop the sexual assault and abuse of young innocent boys in the Catholic Church if we don't look at it for what it really is? These men of the cloth who are gay pedophiles use their positions to mask their crimes and cover them up. They know that some, not all, members of the LGBTQIA community will protect them in order to serve the greater good, which is sparing the reputation of the LGBTQIA community over seeing to the end of child sexual abuse by gay pedophiles. And that is where I have drawn the line! Heterosexuals, take a stand!

Chapter 18

How Society Has Been Betrayed by the LGBTQIA Community

From tolerance, to equality, to protected class, to equity, to betrayal, to erasing heterosexuality, to heterophobia, What is a woman?

The LGBTQIA community has betrayed the heterosexual community so that they could gain power and then erase heterosexuality into extinction.

Let's start with tolerance. The LGBTQIA community began by saying that all they wanted was for the heterosexual community to tolerate their behavior and to accept them for who they are as people. The LGBTQIA community said that they just wanted to be accepted and allowed to live their lives without being discriminated against, bullied, or targeted for violence.

They said, "What we do in our bedrooms is our business." This was the gateway to being accepted in society. They said, "Just leave us alone and let us live our lives." Then more and more, heterosexuals started to accept the LGBTQIA community as a whole.

They gained a lot of support from tolerance. They got jobs, bank loans, and housing without being discriminated against. Then they got to celebrate their community with a nationwide Pride Day parade.

Then they were afforded the right, through a Supreme Court decision, to get married as same-sex couples. There is nothing wrong with any of the social advances the LGBTQIA community has made.

Now let's look at equality. The LGBTQIA community has gone from asking for tolerance to wanting to be seen as equal in society and equal to heterosexuals. This resulted in other sorts of things, such as workplaces agreeing to pay for gay and lesbian couples to adopt children. This was the beginning of accepting all things gay. Once gay adoption was implemented in society, the LGBTQIA movement picked up steam and the heterosexual community lost their grip on requirements for those who are in positions to teach their children values and what they were permitted to teach. So, whose values do the children internalize, homosexuals' or heterosexuals.' This is where heterosexuals should have drawn the line. Why? Because now heterosexuals have lost the battle over who instills their own children with values, their children having been placed in the hands of the LGBTQIA community. Which is not what the heterosexuals wanted. By being passive and afraid to address the issue for fear of backlash from the LGBTQIA community, and by not pushing back and insisting on their right to raise their own children and instill them with their own set of values, the heterosexual community in essence surrendered, turning a blind eye to the actions of the gatekeepers of the LGBTQIA community. Which was a major mistake. Why? Because now many members inthe LGBTQIA community want everything they believe in to be accepted, including a homosexual sex ed curriculum for first graders, which also includes drag queens putting on a striptease show for children, the introduction of children's books that talk about and describe gay sex, the rise of health-care providers in schools giving children advice and guidance for the use of puberty blockers without their parents' consent, and schools providing information about and guidance for experimental gender reassignment surgery, meaning that a minor child can decide all on his or her own, without parental consent, to have permanent sex-change surgery. That's just the beginning of the insanity, all in the name of so-called "equality."

Now let's look at the protected class status. Why is the LGBTQIA community being protected by the states, the federal government, and business entities, when the heterosexual community is not? What makes them special and better than us? The answer is nothing! The states, the federal government, and business entities are protecting the LGBTQIA community because they know that this is a community that in most cases(not all) engages in groupthink. Groupthink is a way to get a message across to a massive number of people. By encouraging groupthink, the LGBTQIA community can manipulate and control their members through the mainstream media and social media with a single message, whether the message is true or not. There are plenty of messages, such as those on climate change and COVID-19, that are highly controversial, and each has its truths and its lies. However, the majority(not all) of the LGBTQIA community has remained staunchly on one side of the political aisle. They stay in lockstep with the leftists. Why? Because they have been told to believe what the Democrats say and not even listen to the Republicans.

So, why are the members of the LGBTQIA community listening to only one political party? It's because, given that there is no such thing as something for nothing, they have to pay the Democrats back for the favors they have given them. It comes down to "We will protect you and give you special status if you listen to us, agree with us, buy what we are selling, and vote our way." It's quid pro quo, a.k.a. a bribe. The leftists have brainwashed (not all) but many members of the LGBTQIA community with their single-minded message. They also pump into their heads whatever message that they want to because they know that many members (not all) of the LGBTQIA community will believe anything they say. Why? Because the brainwashing has taken effect *not* to listen to or believe anyone but them. Therefore, these people never reach out to the other side to compare the messages and see if the entities pretending to support them are lying to them. That's why it's brainwashing. Now these entities, the states, the federal government, and the big businesses, can spread whatever message they want among the LGBTQIA community, who will fall in line like a cult. Why do I say like a cult? Because a cult leader brainwashes cult members in the same manner. The key is to isolate them and make them listen to *only* the cult leader, disregarding everyone else's messages, and then they will do whatever they are told without even challenging or questioning the leader. They'll just fall in line, *even though it's not in their best interests*. That's the key to a cult. Leaders get the members to go against their own best interests and to fall in line, following the messages of their so-called "leader." This is all by design. In today's society, it's a case of show favor to the LGBTQIA community in some way, then have them listen to *only* your message and, at the same time, demonize the other side's message as untrue. Then have them fall in line, even if what you're telling them is a lie or goes against their own best interests, and then you have yourself some cult members for life—unless they are deprogrammed to return from the hypnotic state they are in. The leftists like to put everyone into a group rather than reckon with them as individuals. Why? Because then they can control them with cultlike tactics.

Now let's look at equity. What is so-called "equity"? *Equity* sounds a lot like *equality*, but it's really the total opposite.

Equality means that everyone has the same opportunity, even though some people are better than others. Therefore, there will be a different outcome, because some people's abilities and skills are better than others', and we want the best of the best to strive and to lead our great nation. Equity on the other hand, even though it sounds the same, is a total disaster. Why? Because even though we want people to have the same opportunities to strive and achieve, so-called "equity" will hurt the strongest and the best, which will ultimately hurt our great nation and destroy its core. With equity as a social policy, all the underachievers, misfits, and losers will realize the same outcome as those with great achievements. It is totally unfair to the people who worked hard to achieve greatness to give them the same outcome as the slackers or underachievers receive.

With equity as a social policy, it means that a lot of unqualified people will be running our businesses and our country. This means that businesses will fail and the United States will lose its prominence on the world stage, which will allow lesser nations to triumph over us and our enemies to destroy us.

Now why would the leftists want equity rather than equality? Because with equity, you can give the underachievers, and in this instance the LGBTQIA community, a helping hand and a leg up, affording them special privileges and preferential treatment that heterosexuals do not get. Why provide these things to the LGBQTIA community? Because now they are a loyal cultlike member who will do anything that you say or ask of them without challenging you or questioning your authority—even if what you are asking goes against their best interests or is just plain wrong. So, being part of a so-called "protected class" equals being a lifetime member of something that is much like a cult. Now I know that some readers will call me out for saying that the LGBTQIA community is like a cult. It's homophobic and offensive, right? Well, you would be right on cue, making my point for me, namely that you will listen to only the leaders and not even question them, demonize anyone who challenges their cultlike authority, and then play the sympathetic bully to get the alphabet mob and others to try to silence me or intimidate me. Just the way it was designed by the leftist cultlike leadership.

While I thank you for making my point, it will not stop me from speaking the facts and stating the truth. Sorry, the sympathetic bully tactic is not going to work. I won't shut up! Onto the next topic: betrayal.

How and why did the LGBTQIA community betray the heterosexual community? The LGBTQIA community betrayed the heterosexual community by asking for one thing, "All we want is tolerance," but then having other plans, namely, get the heterosexual community to accept them, which would lead to an equal playing field, and then they'd be able to take over society. Is that not what we see today? Sure it is. Deception was the key to the takeover. Today we live in a society where many members of the LGBTQIA community can't or won't define what a woman is. Why? It's because they want their definition of a woman to be the standard along with their version of a woman, neither of which leaves room for the heterosexual woman. What's their definition of a woman? A transgender woman, that is, a biological male who identifies as a woman—and this is the way to erase traditional heterosexual women off the map.

The LGBTQIA community has had other support for their cause that enabled them to carry out this takeover. Now we have politicians and other government leaders who pretend that they can't define what is a woman. Also, these same LGBTQIA community leaders and members are saying that a man can get pregnant and are calling heterosexual women "birthing people," again waging a war on heterosexual women, seeking to erase them from existence. Also, members of the LGBTQIA community play the sympathetic bully as though they are above being questioned, challenged, or opposed. And if they are, they will smear, shame, intimidate the person who is challenging them and try to destroy that individual's life simply for not agreeing with them and supporting their agenda. So much for so-called "tolerance." Also, the LGBTQIA community betrayed heterosexual parents. How? Well, initially the LGBTQIA community said to the heterosexual community, "Stay out of our bedrooms." Now members of the LGBTQIA community are bringing their bedrooms into our heterosexual children's classrooms. They want to teach our innocent and impressionable children, through drag queen story hour, about homosexuality. They want to teach our innocent and impressionable children a sexual curriculum by using books chosen by the LGBTQIA community. They want to have our innocent and impressionable children keep secrets and *not* tell us as the parents. They want your child to identify as the opposite gender and/or permanently change his or her gender. In other words, LGBTQIA teachers persuade students, saying things such as, "Do not tell your parents that you are now a girl after you left home this morning as a boy." The LGBTQIA community wants to have teacher, and not you as a parent, teaching your young, innocent, and impressionable children about sex, including homosexual sex. This is a *betrayal at the highest level.* Also, school is the perfect breeding ground for pedophiles and the easiest place to gain access to children, which puts your young, innocent, and impressionable children at risk of being sexually assaulted. Betrayal is what this is. So much for "stay out of my bedroom."

Now let's look at the erasing of heterosexuality. If the LGBTQIA community can catch children at a very young age and, without parental oversight or permission, get them to change their gender by way of "gender-affirming" or gender-reassignment surgery and treatment, then those children will eventually wipe out the heterosexual community, within two to three generations, by becoming part of the LGBTQIA community and encouraging those who come after them to do the same. It's a betrayal at the highest level, designed by the LGBTQIA community to erase heterosexuality. They are going after the most innocent among us, heterosexual children, by lying to them and claiming that they are trans kids even at the grade schools level. By labeling them as trans kids, they can indoctrinate them more easily, as they already have the brainwashing tools to spark the conversation. This "trans kid" label gives members of the LGBTQIA community access to the minds of children, which now they can manipulate and twist and mold like clay, shutting out their parents' values and instilling the values of the LGBTQIA community.

How is it that this manipulation is able to work? Because the children's parents aren't there on the school ground to counter the brainwashing, which is the whole reason the LGBTQIA community doesn't want the parents' involvement and also the reason why they want the schoolchildren to keep this sexual secret from their parents. Schools with zero parent involvement are the perfect recruitment and indoctrination camps for the LGBTQIA community. Heterosexual community, you may no longer be considered offensive or called homophobic. That's the LGBTQIA community's way of keeping you at bay so that you won't challenge them or even question them, thereby allowing them to complete the recruitment and indoctrination of your heterosexual children, turning them gay and turning them against your heterosexual values and beliefs. It's time to stand up for your children and your own heterosexual existence and confront this betrayal.

So, what happened to tolerance, equality, and "stay out of my bedroom"? I guess it wasn't good enough to erase the heterosexual community from existence. So, why did the LGBTQIA community drop their pursuit of tolerance, equality, and "stay out of my bedroom" and go on this takeover quest? Because this was their deceptive plan all along. We gave them an inch, and they took a mile. Now we are the ones who are being bullied and pushed into the closet. If the LGBTQIA community says any differently, then what they are trying to get us to believe is that the agenda they have in place right now for schools and society as a whole happened just by chance. No way in hell! This was planned, just as it was plotted to erase heterosexuality into extinction. The proof is that this plan is in effect right now as I write this, July 24, 2023, at 4:36 p.m.

Now let's look at heterophobia. Heterophobia involves intimidation of, bullying of, and discrimination against heterosexual people just because they don't agree with the LGBTQIA community's lifestyle or agenda. What happened to "let's agree to disagree"? The LGBTQIA community wants the heterosexual community to agree with them on every issue that they deem important, and if they don't, they call them homophobic. As the LGBTQIA community says, we as a society must celebrate Pride Day. In other words, you must celebrate the LGBTQIA community or else you are homophobic. Given this fact, the heterosexual community has no choice but to embrace the LGBTQIA lifestyle. I respectfully disagree because I have my own thoughts, my own points of view, and my own opinions, and I'm entitled to them all. And no one can bully me into submission. So, who has the real phobia? It's the members of LGBTQIA community who think this way.

Someone who tells me that I don't have the right to disagree with them is heterophobic whether they are a member of the LGBTQIA community or not. Now why do they believe they have the right to take away my rights? Because of one thing and one thing only: because they are a protected class, they believe they are privileged and entitled over the heterosexual community. Which makes them the real heterophobes. Again, what happened to tolerance, equality, and "stay out of my bedroom"? It means nothing when you have a plan to take over society, erase heterosexuality entirely, and try to bully heterosexuals into the closet by using heterophobic tactics!

Chapter 19

LGBTQIA—the So-Called "Protected Class" over Heterosexuals

Why is the LGBTQIA community a so-called "protected class" over the heterosexual community? Why do their rights trump others' rights in a head-to-head sort of situation? Why are other groups or communities getting involved in the LGBTQIA movement? I'll tell you why. It's because they are using the LGBTQIA community like the LGBTQIA community uses black people, to bolster their case as so-called "victims." It's easier to get behind a politically correct movement than it is to go it alone. Now everyone who is in the victim category can be protected and get special privileges. In other words, there is no accountability for anyone who claims to be "offended" or a "victim." Now everyone who claims to be a victim can be a sympathetic bully and control and dictate to the strong and more powerful, bringing them down to silence and censor them and make them bow down to the sympathetic bully's will. That's how these people have weakened the country, by weakening themselves and then somehow turning their weaknesses into a strength. Now the underachievers and the weak have all the power. Therefore, everyone wants to be in a protected class. Why? Because there is power in a protected class, including to take down the heterosexual community as a whole. The process has already started. Now, heterosexuals, what are you going to do about it?

Chapter 20

The Backlash Has Begun. Enough Is Enough! Heterosexuals, It's Time to Take a Stand or Be Bullied and Forced into the Closet to Have Your Rights Taken Away

Enough is enough! I have had enough betrayal by the LGBTQIA community. I have had enough of their bullying and their forcing their identity and ideology down my throat and the throats of the heterosexual community. We were told by the LGBTQIA community to stay out of their bedrooms, and we did that. However, we failed to pay heed to two sayings: "If you give them an inch, they'll take a mile" and "If you give a mouse a cookie, then it will ask for some milk." I'm not calling the LGBTQIA community a mouse; it's just a metaphor. However, I am saying that these same LGBTQIA members who asked us to stay out of their bedrooms are now coming into our houses and trying to indoctrinate our children. They're also doing this through the schools and in other areas of society. This will not be tolerated. Heterosexuals are not bothering the LGBTQIA community, so they shouldn't bother us. I will determine what my children's values are and not the LGBTQIA community. However, if they insist on meddling in my family affairs, then I will have no choice but to meddle in their affairs. I come from a mindset of, Sticks and stones may break my bones, but names will never hurt me. So, calling me names such as "homophobic" will not work with me. I'm going to look out for my own values and do what's in the best interests of my children and the rest of my family.

Heterosexuals are saying enough of legally regarding the LGBTQIA community as a protected class, because they are using that status to discriminate against and bully heterosexuals, and to recruit and indoctrinate heterosexual children, while trying to force all heterosexuals into the closet, someplace they refused to stay themselves. From child recruitment and indoctrination in grade schools, to transgender biological males in girls' or women's sports and locker rooms, to parents of students at school board meetings being called domestic terrorists, to an LGBTQIA sexualized curriculum for grade school children, to corporate America employing transgender spokespeople and other replacements for heterosexuals, to young Gen Z boys moving toward conservativeness and away from liberal progressiveness in high schools, and to the LGBTQIA community's woke agenda for our society, the backlash has begun. "We're not going take it anymore!" is what the heterosexual community is saying to the LGBTQIA community. "We are going to take our lives back from the LGBTQIA community oppressors who have betrayed us. Enough is enough!"

Heterosexuals are sick and tired of their rights being taken away from them, making them second-class citizens, with their rights given over to the LGBTQIA community. The LGBTQIA community has deemed themselves the righteous ones over heterosexuals, and they believe that no one has the right to challenge them, oppose them, debate them, or even question them, even if there are wrong or are acting in such a way to oppress heterosexuals. Many members of the LGBTQIA community try to shame heterosexuals and bully them into complying when they don't get their way. Now the heterosexual community is taking a stand and is saying to the LGBTQIA community, "Enough is enough! Who the hell do you think you are? We are not your subordinates, and you are not our bosses. We will take no more of your bullying or oppression!" The heterosexual community doesn't owe the LGBTQIA community anything. Heterosexuals are saying to the LGBTQIA community, "We are taking our lives back. So, if we have to protest, boycott, or vote you out of office, then that's what we will do. Enough is enough!"

Let's start with parents at school board meetings at grade schools that are implementing an LGBTQIA sexualized curriculum and planting LGBTIA books in their classrooms and libraries, while at the same time excluding faith-based books. This plot is part of a grassroots plan to erase heterosexuality and to bully heterosexuals into the closet.

Next up is the issue of biological girls versus transgender girls, that is, biological males who identify is girls. Next is big business in the United States. Next is conservative Generation Z high school boys, many of whom are starting to lean more toward the conservative side and away from the progressive side because of all the attacks on "toxic masculinity" and the silencing and censoring of them, along with their being the target of much abuse, including from the LGBTQIA community. Heterosexuals are taking a stand on all these issues, which matter to them, and more.

ABOUT THE AUTHOR

I wrote *The LGBTQIA Community and Betrayal* because I believe that everyone needs checks and balances, yet no one up to this point has put a check on the LGBTQIA community, likely fearing the alphabet mob's vicious attacks, which are LGBTQIA-orchestrated attacks meant to silence and censor the heterosexual community and discourage them from pushing back or defending themselves. Also, I am concerned about the protected class status of the LGBTQIA community, which gives them unchecked power and the authority to tear down heterosexuality at will and replace it with LGBTQIA homosexuality and the LGBTQIA community's way of thinking, leaving heterosexuals no voice and without representation.

I wrote *The LGBTQIA Community and Betrayal* because the LGBTQIA community has betrayed the trust of the heterosexual community. They are taking away heterosexual parents' rights. They are recruiting and indoctrinating our children, and they are trying to bully us into the closet. I am tired of not being able to voice my thoughts and express my opinions, which I'm entitled to do, just like millions of other heterosexuals. I feel that someone has to step up and speak out in order to preserve the freedom of heterosexuals and end the LGBTQIA community's oppression of us. They are discriminatory, disrespectful, and dishonest toward the heterosexual community. Someone has to be the fact-checker. I believe that I am qualified because in my previous two books I fact-check the feminist movement and the women's movement.

There is a *Millennium Women's War on Men Bully Tactics,* which is why their independence is failing them in their relationships and how to be empowered. *Millennium Women and Gender Assassination,* the plot to destroy all things male. are also engaged in gender assassination and the plot to destroy all things male.

Another reason I wrote *The LGBTQIA Community and Betrayal* is that I literally had a defining, life-changing thing happen to me on the morning of Sunday, August 20, 2023. I woke up around five o'clock in the morning and ran some bathwater as soaking in the tub helps me to think and relax. However, this day my body started to cramp all over because I was dehydrated. This had happened to me plenty of times before, but this time something was different. The cramping would not stop no matter what I did, such as stretch, or how much water I drank. My entire body was cramping from head to toe. I was in the bathroom with the door closed, and the next thing I knew, I was getting up off the floor, as I was lying in a pool of my own blood. This had never happened to me before. I looked into the mirror and saw a gash on my forehead as if something had cut me. I have a television in my bathroom, and the remote control for it was in the pool of blood alongside me, with other items. I felt absolutely no head pain, and I still don't know what happened to me that day.

When I got up, I was bleeding from my nose. That's where the pool of blood had come from, which I just started to wipe up. Then I noticed that I could barely move my arms and my legs. I looked at the clock and saw that three hours had passed. I had lost those three hours of my life, having no memory of them. Then something clicked and I immediately knew that something had happened to me. I don't know why it happened, but I knew that it had happened. In other words, I didn't just pass out: I literally died. I passed away. And the stiffness in my legs and arms, preventing me from moving them, was the result of rigor mortis having started to set in because of lack of oxygen. Therefore, I concluded that I must have stopped breathing for those three hours. My throat was very sore. It had felt like it had shrunk and closed up. I couldn't swallow the simplest thing such as cup of water. However after I got up off the floor, I realized that for some reason God had restored me and given me my life back. I couldn't explain it. It took two and a half weeks for my body to fully recover from the stiffness and for my throat to stop feeling sore. All of a sudden I started to get these loud message in my head, which I knew were from God: "Finish the book on the LGBTQIA community and betrayal."

This was God telling that my purpose and my calling was to finished *The LGBTQIA Community and Betrayal*. He said that he was going to use me to carry out his Word, deliver his message, and carry out his will. I know that some people don't believe in God. I'm not one of them. I know that a miracle happened to me that day. I know that I passed away on my bathroom floor and that God literally brought me back to life. I can't explain it, and I can't ignore his Word or his will. It's like when he used Moses, telling him to go to Pharaoh and say to him, "Let my people go!" I'm not comparing myself to Moses. However, I am saying that God instructed me to write *The LGBTQIA Community and Betrayal* the way that it is written, as these are his words. He wants humankind, meaning his people, not to accept the homosexual lifestyle, because it is *not of his will*. I'm just a messenger who is following the will of God. It's up to the people to listen. He told me to write *The LGBTQIA Community and Betrayal* in order to expose the evil that is being put on the heterosexual community and to give those who are afraid a voice with which to speak up and express their opinions. God chose me as his messenger because he knows that I'm not afraid to express my feelings or opinions or to use my voice.

Therefore, no one can intimidate me, threaten me, shame me, or do anything that will get me to stop delivering his messages and carrying out his will, because I have a higher calling. I have already died and, through a miracle and the grace of God, was brought back to life. So, "no weapon formed against me shall prosper." And if God is for me, then who can be against me?

Printed in the United States
by Baker & Taylor Publisher Services